Hard Press

LONDON IN 1731

by Don Manoel Gonzales

INTRODUCTION.

Don Manoel Gonzales is the assumed name of the writer of a "Voyage to Great Britain, containing an Account of England and Scotland," which was first printed in the first of the two folio volumes of "A Collection of Voyages and Travels, compiled from the Library of the Earl of Oxford" (Robert Harley, who died in 1724, but whose industry in collection was continued by his son Edward, the second Earl), "interspersed and illustrated with Notes." These volumes, known as the "Harleian Collection," were published in 1745 and 1746. The narrative was reproduced early in the present century in the second of the seventeen quartos of John Pinkerton's "General Collection of the best and the most interesting Voyages and Travels of the World" (1808-1814), from which this account of London is taken. The writer does here, no doubt, keep up his character of Portuguese by a light allusion to "our extensive city of Lisbon," but he forgets to show his nationality when speaking of Portugal among the countries with which London has trade, and he writes of London altogether like one to the City born, when he describes its inner life together with its institutions and its buildings.

The book is one of those that have been attributed to Defoe, who died in 1731, and the London it describes was dated by Pinkerton in the last year of Defoe's life. This is also the latest date to be found in the narrative. On page 93 of this volume, old buildings at St. Bartholomew's are said to have been pulled down in the year 1731, "and a magnificent pile erected in the room of them, about 150 feet in length, faced with a pure white stone, besides other additions now building." That passage was written, therefore, after 1731, and could not possibly have been written by Defoe. But if the book was in Robert Harley's collection, and not one of the additions made by his son the second earl, the main body of the account of London must be of a date earlier than the first earl's death in 1724. Note, for instance, the references on pages 27, 28, to "the late Queen Mary," and to "her Majesty" Queen Anne, as if Anne were living. It would afterwards have been brought to date of publication by additions made in or before 1745. The writer, whoever he may have been, was an able man, who joined to the detail of a guide-book the clear observation of one who writes like an educated and not untravelled London merchant, giving a description of his native town as it was in the reign of George the First, with addition of a later touch or two from the beginning of the reign of George the Second.

His London is London of the time when Pope published his translation of the "Iliad," and was nettled at the report that Addison, at Button's Coffee House, had given to Tickell's little venture in the same direction the praise of having more in it of Homer's fire. Button's Coffee House was of Addison's foundation, for the benefit of Daniel Button, an old steward of the Countess of Warwick's, whom he had settled there in 1812. It was in Russell Street, Covent Garden, and Addison brought the wits to it by using it himself. "Don Manoel Gonzales" describes very clearly in the latter part of this account of London, the manner of using taverns and coffee-houses by the Londoners of his days, and other ways of life with high and low. It is noticeable, however, that his glance does not include the ways of men of letters. His four orders of society are, the noblemen and gentlemen, whose wives breakfast at twelve; the merchants and richer tradesmen; after whom he places the lawyers and doctors; whose professional class is followed by that of the small tradesmen, costermongers, and other people of the lower orders. This, and the clearness of detail upon London commerce, may strengthen the general impression that the description comes rather from a shrewd, clear-headed, and successful merchant than from a man of letters.

The London described is that of Addison who died in 1719, of Steele who died in 1729, of Pope who died in 1744. It is the London into which Samuel Johnson came in 1738, at the age of twenty-nine—seven years before the manuscript of "Manoel de Gonzales" appeared in print. "How different a place," said Johnson, "London is to different people; but the intellectual man is struck with it as comprehending the whole of human life in all its variety, the contemplation of which is inexhaustible." Its hard features were shown in the poem entitled London—an imitation of the third satire of Juvenal—with which Johnson began his career in the great city, pressed by poverty, but not to be subdued:-

"By numbers here from shame or censure free,
All crimes are safe but hated poverty.
This, only this, the rigid law pursues,
This, only this, provokes the snarling Muse.
The sober trader, at a tattered cloak,
Wakes from his dream and labours for a joke;
With brisker air the silken courtiers gaze,
And turn the varied taunt a thousand ways.
Of all the griefs that harass the distressed,
Sure the most bitter is a scornful jest;
Fate never wounds more deep the generous heart
Than when a blockhead's insult points the dart."

When Don Manoel's account of London was written the fashionable world was only beginning to migrate from Covent Garden—once a garden belonging to the Convent of Westminster, and the first London square inhabited by persons of rank and fashion—to Grosvenor Square, of which Don Manoel describes the new glories. They included a gilt equestrian statue of King George I. in the middle of its garden, to say nothing of kitchen areas to its houses, then unusual enough to need special description: "To the kitchens and offices, which have little paved yards with vaults before them, they descend by twelve or fifteen steps, and these yards are defended by a high palisade of iron." Altogether, we are told, Grosvenor Square "may well be looked upon as the beauty of the town, and those who have not seen it cannot have an adequate idea of the place."

But Covent Garden is named by "Don Manoel Gonzales," with St. James's Park, as a gathering-place of the London world of fashion. The neighbouring streets, it may be added, had many coffee-houses, wine-cellars, fruit and jelly shops; fruit, flowers, and herbs were sold in its central space; and one large woman thoughtfully considering the fashion of the place, sat at her stall in a lace dress of which the lowest estimate was that it must have cost a hundred guineas.

H. M.

London in 1731.
Containing A *description of the city of London; both in regard to its extent, buildings, government, trade, etc.*

London, the capital of the kingdom of England, taken in its largest extent, comprehends the cities of London and Westminster, with their respective suburbs, and the borough of Southwark, with the buildings contiguous thereto on the south side of the river, both on the east and west sides of the bridge.

The length thereof, if we measure in a direct line from Hyde Park gate, on the west side of Grosvenor Square, to the farthest buildings that are contiguous in Limehouse, that is, from west to east, is very near five miles in a direct line; but if we take in the turnings and windings of the streets, it cannot be less than six miles. The breadth in many places from north to south is about two miles and a half, but in others not above a mile and a half; the circumference of the whole being about sixteen miles.

The situation next the river is hilly, and in some places very steep; but the streets are for the most part upon a level, and the principal of them nowhere to be paralleled for their length, breadth, beauty, and regularity of the buildings, any more than the spacious and magnificent squares with which this city abounds.

As to the dimensions of the city within the walls, I find that the late wall on the land side from the Tower in the east, to the mouth of Fleet Ditch in the west, was two miles wanting ten poles; and the line along the Thames, where there has been no walls for many hundred years, if ever, contains from the Tower in the east, to the mouth of the same ditch in the west, a mile and forty poles; which added to the circuit of the wall, on the land side, makes in the whole three miles thirty poles; and as it is of an irregular figure, narrow at each end, and the broadest part not half the length of it, the content of the ground within the walls, upon the most accurate survey, does not contain more than three hundred and eighty acres; which is not a third part of the contents of our extensive city of Lisbon: but then this must be remembered, Lisbon contains a great quantity of arable and waste ground within its walls, whereas London is one continued pile of buildings. The city gates are at this day eight, besides posterns, *viz.*: 1, Aldgate; 2, Bishopsgate; 3, Moorgate; 4, Cripplegate; 5, Aldersgate; 6, Newgate; 7, Ludgate; and, 8, The Bridgegate.

1. Aldgate, or Ealdgate, in the east, is of great antiquity, even as old as the days of King Edgar, who mentions it in a charter to the knights of Knighton-Guild. Upon the top of it, to the eastward, is placed a golden sphere; and on the upper battlements, the figures of two soldiers as sentinels: beneath, in a large square, King James I. is represented standing in gilt armour, at whose feet are a lion and unicorn, both couchant, the first the supporter of England, and the other for Scotland. On the west side of the gate is the figure of Fortune, finely gilded and carved, with a prosperous sail over her head, standing on a globe, overlooking the city. Beneath it is the King's arms, with the usual motto, Dieu et mon droit, and under it, Vivat rex. A little lower,

on one side, is the figure of a woman, being the emblem of peace, with a dove in one hand, and a gilded wreath or garland in the other; and on the other side is the figure of charity, with a child at her breast, and another in her hand; and over the arch of the gate is this inscription, *viz.*, Senatus populusque Londinensis fecit, 1609, and under it, Humphrey Weld, Mayor, in whose mayoralty it was finished.

2. Bishopsgate, which stands north-west of Aldgate, is supposed to have been built by some bishop about the year 1200. It was afterwards several times repaired by the merchants of the Hanse Towns, on account of the confirmation of their privileges in this city. The figures of the two bishops on the north side are pretty much defaced, as are the city arms engraven on the south side of it.

3. Aldersgate, the ancient north gate of the city, stands to the westward of Bishopsgate. On the north, or outside of it, is the figure of King James I. on horseback, who entered the city at this gate when he came from Scotland, on his accession to the throne of England. Over the head of this figure are the arms of England, Scotland, and Ireland; and on one side the image of the prophet Jeremy, with this text engraved, "Then shall enter into the gates of this city, kings and princes sitting on the throne of David, riding on chariots and on horses, they and their princes, the men of Judah, and the inhabitants of Jerusalem." And on the other side, the figure of the prophet Samuel, with the following passage, "And Samuel said unto all Israel, Behold, I have hearkened unto your voice in all that you have said unto me, and have made a king over you." On the south, or inside of the gate, is the effigy of King James I. sitting on his throne in his robes.

4. Newgate, so called from its being built later than the other principal gates, is situated on the north-west corner of the city, said to be erected in the reign of Henry I. or King Stephen, when the way through Ludgate was interrupted by enlarging the cathedral of St. Paul's and the churchyard about it. This gate hath been the county jail for Middlesex at least five hundred years. The west, or outside of the gate is adorned with three ranges of pilasters and their entablements of the Tuscan order. Over the lowest is a circular pediment, and above it the King's arms. The inter columns are four niches, and as many figures in them, well carved, and large as the life. The east, or inside of the gate, is adorned with a range of pilasters with entablements as the other, and in three niches are the figures of justice, mercy, and truth, with this inscription, *viz.*, "This part of Newgate was begun to be repaired in the mayoralty of Sir James Campel, Knight, anno 1630, and finished in the mayoralty of Sir Robert Ducie, Bart., anno 1631; and being damnified by the fire in 1666, it was repaired in the mayoralty of Sir George Waterman, anno 1672."

5. Ludgate, the ancient western gate of the city, stands between Newgate and the Thames, built by King Lud about threescore years before the birth of our Saviour. It was repaired in the reign of King John, anno 1215, and afterwards in the year 1260, when it was adorned with the figures of King Lud and his two sons, Androgeus and Theomantius; but at the Reformation, in the reign of Edward VI., some zealous people struck off all their heads, looking upon images of all kinds to be Popish and idolatrous. In the reign of Queen Mary, new heads were placed on the bodies of

these kings, and so remained till the 28th of Queen Elizabeth, anno 1586, when the gate, being very ruinous, was pulled down, and beautifully rebuilt: the east or inside whereof was adorned with four pilasters and entablature of the Doric order, and in the intercolumns were placed the figures of King Lud and his two sons (who are supposed to have succeeded him) in their British habits again; and above them the queen's arms, *viz.*, those of France and England quarterly, the supporters a lion and a dragon. It was afterwards repaired and beautified, anno 1699, Sir Francis Child lord mayor. The west or outside of the gate is adorned with two pilasters and entablature of the Ionic order; also two columns and a pediment adorning a niche, wherein is placed a good statue of Queen Elizabeth in her robes and the regalia; and over it the queen's arms between the city supporters, placed at some distance. This gate was made a prison for debtors who were free of the city, anno 1 Richard II., 1378, Nicholas Brember then mayor, and confirmed such by the mayor and common council, anno 1382, John Northampton mayor.

The Tower of London is situated at the south-east end of the city, on the river Thames, and consists in reality of a great number of towers or forts, built at several times, which still retain their several names, though at present most of them, together with a little town and church, are enclosed within one wall and ditch, and compose but one entire fortress.

It was the vulgar opinion that the Tower was built by Julius Cæsar; but, as I have before shown, history informs us that Cæsar made no stay in England, that he erected no town or fortress, unless that with which he enclosed his ships on the coast of Kent, nor left a single garrison or soldier in the island on his departure.

This Tower, as now encompassed, stands upon twelve acres of ground, and something more, being of an irregular form, but approaching near to that of an oblong, one of the longest sides lying next the river, from whence it rises gradually towards the north, by a pretty deep ascent, to the armoury, which stands upon the highest ground in the Tower, overlooking the White Tower built by William the Conqueror, and the remains of the castle below it on the Thames side, said to be built by William Rufus.

As to the strength of the place, the works being all antique, would not be able to hold out four-and-twenty hours against an army prepared for a siege: the ditch indeed is of a great depth, and upwards of a hundred feet broad, into which the water of the Thames may be introduced at pleasure; but I question whether the walls on the inside would bear the firing of their own guns: certain it is, two or three battering-pieces would soon lay them even with the ground, though, after all, the ditch alone is sufficient to defend it against a sudden assault. There are several small towers upon the walls; those of the largest dimensions, and which appear the most formidable, are the Divelin Tower, on the north-west; and the Martin Tower on the north-east; and St. Thomas's Tower on the river by Traitor's Bridge; which I take to be part of the castle said to be built by William Rufus. There is also a large tower on the outside the ditch, called the Lions' Tower, on the south-west corner, near which is the principal gate and bridge by which coaches and carriages enter the Tower; and there are two posterns with bridges over the ditch to the wharf on the Thames side, one whereof is called Traitor's Bridge, under which state prisoners used to enter the Tower.

The principal places and buildings within the Tower, are (1) The parochial church of St. Peter (for the Tower is a parish of itself, in which are fifty houses and upwards, inhabited by the governor, deputy-governor, warders, and other officers belonging to the fortress).

(2) To the eastward of the church stands a noble pile of building, usually called the armoury, begun by King James II. and finished by King William III., being three hundred and ninety feet in length, and sixty in breadth: the stately door-case on the south side is adorned with four columns, entablature and triangular pediment, of the Doric order. Under the pediment are the king's arms, with enrichments of trophy-work, very ornamental. It consists of two lofty rooms, reaching the whole length of the building: in the lower room is a complete train of artillery, consisting of brass cannon and mortars fit to attend an army of a hundred-thousand men; but none of the cannon I observe there were above four-and-twenty pounders; the large battering-pieces, which carry balls of thirty-two and forty-eight pounds weight, I perceive, are in the king's store-houses at Deptford, Woolwich, Chatham, and Portsmouth. In the armoury also we find a great many of the little cohorn mortars, so called from the Dutch engineer Cohorn, who invented them for firing a great number of hand-grenades from them at once; with other extraordinary pieces cast at home, or taken from the enemy.

In the room over the artillery is the armoury of small arms, of equal dimensions with that underneath, in which are placed, in admirable order, muskets and other small arms for fourscore thousand men, most of them of the newest make, having the best locks, barrels, and stocks, that can be contrived for service; neither the locks or barrels indeed are wrought, but I look upon them to be the more durable and serviceable, and much easier cleaned. There are abundance of hands always employed in keeping them bright, and they are so artfully laid up, that any one piece may be taken down without moving another. Besides these, which with pilasters of pikes furnish all the middle of the room from top to bottom, leaving only a walk through the middle, and another on each side, the north and south walls of the armoury are each of them adorned with eight pilasters of pikes and pistols of the Corinthian order, whose intercolumns are chequer-work of carbines and pistols; waves of the sea in cutlasses, swords, and bayonets; half moons, semicircles, and a target of bayonets; the form of a battery in swords and pistols; suns, with circles of pistols; a pair of gates in halberts and pistols; the Witch of Endor, as it is called, within three ellipses of pistols; the backbone of a whale in carbines; a fiery serpent, Jupiter and the Hydra, in bayonets, &c. But nothing looks more beautiful and magnificent than the four lofty wreathed columns formed with pistols in the middle of the room, which seem to support it. They show us also some other arms, which are only remarkable for the use they have been put to; as the two swords of state, carried before the Pretender when he invaded Scotland in the year 1715; and the arms taken from the Spaniards who landed in Scotland in the year 1719, &c.

The small arms were placed in this beautiful order by one Mr. Harris, originally a blacksmith, who was properly the forger of his own fortune, having raised himself by his merit: he had a place or pension granted him by the government for this piece of service in particular, which he richly deserved, no nation in Europe being able to show a magazine of small arms so good in their kind, and so ingeniously disposed. In the place where the armoury now stands was formerly a bowling-green, a garden, and some buildings, which were demolished to make room for the grand arsenal I have been describing.

In the horse-armoury the most remarkable things are some of the English kings on horseback in complete armour, among which the chief are Edward III., Henrys V. and VII., King Charles I. and II., and King William, and a suit of silver armour, said to belong to John of Gaunt, seven feet and a half high. Here also they show us the armour of the Lord Kingsale, with the sword he took from the French general, which gained him the privilege of being covered in the king's presence, which his posterity enjoy to this day.

The office of ordnance is in the Tower, with the several apartments of the officers that belong to it, who have the direction of all the arms, ammunition, artillery, magazines, and stores of war in the kingdom.

The White Tower is a lofty, square stone building, with a turret at each angle, standing on the declivity of the hill, a little below the armoury, and disengaged from the other buildings, where some thousand barrels of powder were formerly kept; but great part of the public magazine of powder is now distributed in the several yards and storehouses belonging to the government, as at Woolwich, Chatham, Portsmouth, Plymouth, &c., to prevent accidents, I presume; for should such a prodigious quantity of powder take fire, it must be of fatal consequence to the city, as well as the Tower. The main guard of the Tower, with the lodgings of the officers, are on the east side of this building.

In the chapel of the White Tower, usually called Caesar's Chapel, and in a large room adjoining on the east side thereof, sixty-four feet long, and thirty-one broad, are kept many ancient records, such as privy-seals in several reigns, bills, answers, and depositions in chancery, in the reigns of Queen Elizabeth, King James I., and King Charles I., writs of distringas, supersedeas, de excommunicato capiendo, and other writs relating to the courts of law; but the records of the greatest importance are lodged in the Tower called Wakefield Tower, consisting of statute rolls from the 6th of Edward I. to the 8th of Edward III.

Parliament rolls beginning anno 5 of Edward II. and ending with the reign of Edward IV.

Patent rolls beginning anno 3 of John, and ending with the reign of Edward IV. In these are contained grants of offices, hands, tenements, temporalities, &c., passing under the great seal.

10

Charter rolls, from the 1st of King John to the end of Edward IV. in which are enrolments of grants, and confirmations of liberties and privileges to cities and towns corporate, and to private persons, as markets, fairs, free warren, common of pasture, waifs, strays, felons' goods, &c.

The foundations of abbeys and priories, of colleges and schools, together with lands and privileges granted to them.

The patents of creation of noblemen.

Close rolls, from the 6th of King John, to the end of Edward IV., in which are writs of various kinds, but more especially on the back of the roll are entered the writs of summons to parliament, both to the lords and commons, and of the bishops and inferior clergy to convocations. There are also proclamations, and enrolments of deeds between party and party.

French rolls, beginning anno 1 of Edward II. and ending with Edward IV., in which are leagues and treaties with the kings of France, and other matters relating to that kingdom.

Scotch rolls, containing transactions with that kingdom.

Rome, touching the affairs of that see.

Vascon rolls, relating to Gascoign.

There are also other rolls and records of different natures.

In this tower are also kept the inquisitions post mortem, from the first year of King Henry III., to the third year of Richard III.

The inquisitions ad quod damnum, from the first of Edward II. to the end of Henry V.

Writs of summons, and returns to Parliament, from the reign of Edward I. to the 17th of Edward IV.

Popes' bulls, and original letters from foreign princes.

All which were put into order, and secured in excellent wainscot presses, by order of the house of peers, in the year 1719 and 1720. Attendance is given at this office, and searches may be made from seven o'clock in the morning to eleven, and from one to five in the afternoon, unless in December, January, and February, when the office is open only from eight to eleven in the morning, and from one to four, except holidays.

The next office I shall mention is the Mint, where, at present, all the money in the kingdom is coined. This makes a considerable street in the Tower, wherein are apartments for the officers belonging to it. The principal officers are:- 1. The warden, who receives the gold and silver bullion, and pays the full value for it, the charge being defrayed by a small duty on wines. 2. The master and worker, who takes the bullion from the warden, causes it to be melted, delivers it to the moneyers, and when it is minted receives it from them again. 3. The comptroller, who sees that the money be made according to the just assize, overlooks the officers and controls them. 4. The assay-master, who sees that the money be according to the standard of fineness. 5. The auditor, who takes the accounts, and makes them up. 6. The surveyor-general, who takes care that the fineness be not altered in the melting. And, 7, the weigher and teller.

The Jewel-office, where the regalia are reposited, stands near the east end of the Armoury. A list is usually given to those who come daily to see these curiosities in the Jewel-house, a copy whereof follows, *viz.*:

A list of his Majesty's regalia, besides plate, and other rich things, at the Jewel-house in the Tower of London.

1. The imperial crown, which all the kings of England have been crowned with, ever since Edward the Confessor's time.

2. The orb, or globe, held in the king's left hand at the coronation; on the top of which is a jewel near an inch and half in height.

3. The royal sceptre with the cross, which has another jewel of great value under it.

4. The sceptre with the dove, being the emblem of peace.

5. St. Edward's staff, all beaten gold, carried before the king at the coronation.

6. A rich salt-cellar of state, the figure of the Tower, used on the king's table at the coronation.

7. Curtana, or the sword of mercy, borne between the two swords of justice, the spiritual and temporal, at the coronation.

8. A noble silver font, double gilt, that the kings and royal family were christened in.

9. A large silver fountain, presented to King Charles II. by the town of Plymouth.

10. Queen Anne's diadem, or circlet which her majesty wore in proceeding to her coronation.

11. The coronation crown made for the late Queen Mary.

12. The rich crown of state that his majesty wears on his throne in parliament, in which is a large emerald seven inches round, a pearl the finest in the world, and a ruby of inestimable value.

13. A globe and sceptre made for the late Queen Mary.

14. An ivory sceptre with a dove, made for the late King James's queen.

15. The golden spurs and the armillas that are worn at the coronation.

There is also an apartment in the Tower where noble prisoners used to be confined, but of late years some of less quality have been sent thither.

The Tower where the lions and other savage animals are kept is on the right hand, on the outside the ditch, as we enter the fortress. These consist of lions, leopards, tigers, eagles, vultures, and such other wild creatures as foreign princes or sea-officers have presented to the British kings and queens.

Not far from the Tower stands London Bridge. This bridge has nineteen arches besides the drawbridge, and is built with hewn stone, being one thousand two hundred feet in length, and seventy-four in breadth, whereof the houses built on each side take up twenty-seven feet, and the street between the houses twenty feet; there being only three vacancies about the middle of the bridge where there are no houses, but a low stone wall, with an iron palisade, through which is a fine view of the shipping and vessels in the river. This street over the bridge is as much thronged, and has as brisk a trade as any street in the city; and the perpetual passage of coaches and carriages makes it troublesome walking on it, there being no posts to keep off carriages as in other streets. The middle vacancy was left for a drawbridge, which used formerly to be drawn up when shipping passed that way; but no vessels come above the bridge at this day but such as can strike their masts, and pass under the arches. Four of the arches on the north side of the bridge are now taken up with mills and engines, that raise the water to a great height, for the supply of the city; this brings in a large revenue which, with the rents of the houses on the bridge, and other houses and lands that belong to it, are applied as far as is necessary to the repair of it by the officers appointed for that service, who are, a comptroller and two bridge-masters, with their subordinate officers; and in some years, it is said, not less than three thousand pounds are laid out in repairing and supporting this mighty fabric, though it be never suffered to run much to decay.

I come next to describe that circuit of ground which lies without the walls, but within the freedom and jurisdiction of the City of London. And this is bounded by a line which begins at Temple Bar, and extends itself by many turnings and windings through part of Shear Lane, Bell Yard, Chancery Lane, by the Rolls Liberty, &c., into Holborn, almost against Gray's-Inn Lane, where there is a bar (consisting of posts, rails, and a chain) usually called Holborn Bars; from whence it passes with many turnings and windings by the south end of Brook Street, Furnival's Inn, Leather Lane, the south end of Hatton Garden, Ely House, Field Lane, and Chick Lane, to the common sewer; then to Cow Cross, and so to Smithfield Bars; from whence it runs with several windings between Long Lane and Charterhouse Lane to Goswell Street, and so up that street northward to the Bars.

From these Bars in Goswell Street, where the manor of Finsbury begins, the line extends by Golden Lane to the posts and chain in Whitecross Street, and from thence to the posts and chain in Grub Street; and then runs through Ropemakers Alley to the posts and chain in the highway from Moorgate, and from thence by the north side of Moorfields; after which it runs northwards to Nortonfalgate, meeting with the bars in Bishopsgate Street, and from thence runs eastward into Spittlefields, abutting all along upon Nortonfalgate.

From Nortonfalgate it returns southwards by Spittlefields, and then south-east by Wentworth Street, to the bars in Whitechapel. From hence it inclines more southerly to the Little Minories and Goodman's Fields: from whence it returns westward to the posts and chain in the Minories, and so on more westerly till it comes to London Wall, abutting on the Tower Liberty, and there it ends. The ground comprehended betwixt this line and the city wall contains about three hundred acres.

There is no wall or fence, as has been hinted already, to separate the freedom of the City from that part of the town which lies in the county of Middlesex, only posts and chains at certain places, and one gate at the west end of Fleet Street which goes by the name of Temple Bar.

This gate resembles a triumphal arch; it is built of hewn stone, each side being adorned with four pilasters, their entablature, and an arched pediment of the Corinthian order. The intercolumns are niches replenished; those within the Bar towards the east, with the figures of King James I. and his queen; and those without the Bar, with the figures of King Charles I. and King Charles II. It is encircled also with cornucopias, and has two large cartouches by way of supporters to the whole; and on the inside of the gate is the following inscription, *viz.*, "Erected in the year 1671, Sir Samuel Starling, Mayor: continued in the year 1670, Sir Richard Ford, Lord Mayor: and finished in the year 1672, Sir George Waterman, Lord Mayor."

The city is divided into twenty-six wards or governments, each having its peculiar officers, as alderman, common council, &c. But all are subject to the lord mayor, the supreme magistrate of this great metropolis. Of each of these wards take the following account.

1. Portsoken ward is situate without Aldgate, the most easterly ward belonging to the City; and extends from Aldgate eastward to the bars. The chief streets and places comprehended in it, are part of Whitechapel Street, the Minories, Houndsditch, and the west side of Petticoat Lane.

Whitechapel is a handsome broad street, by which we enter the town from the east. The south side, or great part of it, is taken up by butchers who deal in the wholesale way, selling whole carcases of veal, mutton, and lamb (which come chiefly out of Essex) to the town butchers. On the north side are a great many good inns, and several considerable tradesmen's houses, who serve the east part of England with such goods and merchandise as London affords. On the south side is a great market for hay three times a week.

Tower ward extends along the Thames from the Tower on the east almost to Billingsgate on the west, and that part of the Tower itself which lies to the westward of the White Tower is held by some to be within this ward. The principal streets and places contained in it are Great Tower Street, part of Little Tower Street and Tower Hill, part of Thames Street, Mark Lane, Mincing Lane, Seething Lane, St. Olave Hart Street, Idle Lane, St. Dunstan's Hill, Harp Lane, Water Lane, and Bear Lane, with the courts and alleys that fall into them.

Great Tower Hill lies on the outside of the Tower Ditch towards the north-west.

Upon this hill is a scaffold erected, at the charge of the City, for the execution of noble offenders imprisoned in the Tower (after sentence passed upon them).

The names of the quays or wharves lying on the Thames side in this ward between the Tower and Billingsgate, are Brewer's Quay, Chester Quay, Galley Quay, Wool Quay, Porter's Quay, Custom-House Quay, Great Bear Quay, Little Bear Quay, Wigging's Quay, Ralph's Quay, Little Dice Quay, Great Dice Quay, and Smart's Quay, of which, next to the Custom-House Quay, Bear Quays are the most considerable, there being one of the greatest markets in England for wheat and other kinds of grain, brought hither by coasting vessels.

The public buildings in this ward (besides the western part of the Tower above-mentioned to be within the City) are the Custom House, Cloth-workers' Hall, Bakers' Hall, and the three parish churches of Allhallows Barking, St. Olave Hart Street, and St. Dunstan's in the East.

The Custom House is situated on the north side of the Thames, between the Tower and Billingsgate, consisting of two floors, in the uppermost of which, in a wainscoted magnificent room, almost the whole length of the building, and fifteen feet in height, sit the commissioners of the customs, with their under officers and clerks. The length of this edifice is a hundred and eighty-nine feet, and the general breadth twenty-seven, but at the west end it is sixty feet broad. It is built of brick and stone, and covered with lead, being adorned with the upper and lower orders of architecture.

3. Aldgate, or Ealdgate Ward. The principal streets and places in it are Aldgate Street, Berry Street, part of St. Mary Axe, part of Leadenhall Street, part of Lime Street, Billiter Lane and Square, part of Mark Lane, Fenchurch Street, and Crutchedfriars.

The public buildings in this ward are the African House, the Navy Office, Bricklayers' Hall, the churches of St. Catherine Creechurch, St. James's, Duke's Place, St. Andrew Undershaft, St. Catherine Coleman, and the Jews' Synagogues.

The Royal African House is situated on the south side of Leadenhall Street, near the east end of it. Here the affairs of the company are transacted; but the house has nothing in it that merits a particular description.

The Navy Office is situated on the south side of Crutchedfriars, near Tower Hill, being a large, well-built pile of buildings, and the offices for every branch of business relating to the navy admirably well disposed.

The Jews' synagogues are in Duke's Place, where, and in that neighbourhood, many of that religion inhabit. The synagogue stands east and West, as Christian churches usually do: the great door is on the west, within which is a long desk upon an ascent, raised above the floor, from whence the law is read. The east part of the synagogue also is railed in, and the places where the women sit enclosed with lattices; the men sit on benches with backs to them, running east and west; and there are abundance of fine branches for candles, besides lamps, especially in that belonging to the Portuguese.

4. Lime Street Ward. The principal streets and places in it are part of Leadenhall Street, and Leadenhall Market, part of Lime Street, and part of St. Mary Axe.

Leadenhall Market, the finest shambles in Europe, lies between Leadenhall Street and Fenchurch Street. Of the three courts or yards which it consists of, the first is that at the north-east corner of Gracechurch Street, and opens into Leadenhall Street. This court or yard contains in length from north to south 164 feet, and in breadth from east to west eighty feet: within this court or yard, round about the same, are about 100 standing stalls for butchers, for the selling of beef only, and therefore this court is called the beef market. These stalls are either under warehouses, or sheltered from the weather by roofs over them. This yard is on Tuesdays a market for leather, to which the tanners resort; on Thursdays the waggons from Colchester, and other parts, come with baize, &c., and the fellmongers with their wool; and on Fridays it is a market for raw hides; on Saturdays, for beef and other provisions.

The second market yard is called the Greenyard, as being once a green plot of ground; afterwards it was the City's storeyard for materials for building and the like; but now a market only for veal, mutton, lamb, &c. This yard is 170 feet in length from east to west, and ninety feet broad from north to south; it hath in it 140 stalls for the butchers, all covered over. In the middle of this Greenyard market from north to south is a row of shops, with rooms over them, for fishmongers: and on the south side and west end are houses and shops also for fishmongers. Towards the east end of this yard is erected a fair market-house, standing upon columns, with vaults underneath, and rooms above, with a bell tower, and a clock, and under it are butchers' stalls. The tenements round about this yard are for the most part inhabited by cooks and victuallers; and in the passages leading out of the streets into this market are fishmongers, poulterers, cheesemongers, and other traders in provisions.

The third market belonging to Leadenhall is called the Herb Market, for that herbs, roots, fruits, &c., are only there sold. This market is about 140 feet square; the west, east, and north sides had walks round them, covered over for shelter, and standing upon columns; in which walks there were twenty-eight stalls for gardeners, with cellars under them.

The public buildings in this ward are Leadenhall, the East India House, Pewterers' Hall, and Fletchers' Hall.

Leadenhall is situated on the south side of Leadenhall Street. It is a large stone fabric, consisting of three large courts or yards, as has been observed already; part of it is at present a warehouse, in the occupation of the East India Company, where the finest calicoes, and other curiosities of the Eastern part of the world, are reposited; another part of it is for Colchester baize, and is open every Thursday and Friday. Here was also anciently a chapel, and a fraternity of sixty priests constituted to celebrate Divine Service every day to the market people; but was dissolved with other religious societies at the Reformation.

On the south side of Leadenhall Street also, and a little to the eastward of Leadenhall, stands the East India House, lately magnificently built, with a stone front to the street; but the front being very narrow, does not make an appearance answerable to the grandeur of the house within, which stands upon a great deal of ground, the offices and storehouses admirably well contrived, and the public hall and the committee room scarce inferior to anything of the like nature in the City.

There is not one church in this ward at present. The officers of the ward are, an alderman, his deputy, four common-council men, four constables, two scavengers, sixteen for the wardmote inquest, and a beadle.

5. Bishopsgate Ward is divided into two parts, one within Bishopsgate, and the other without.

The streets and places in this ward, within the gate, are, all Bishopsgate Street, part of Gracechurch Street, all Great and Little St. Helen's, all Crosby Square, all Camomile Street, and a small part of Wormwood Street, with several courts and alleys that fall into them.

That part of this ward that lies without Bishopsgate extends northwards as far as the bars, being the bounds of the City freedom on this side.

The principal streets and places in this ward, without the gate, are, Bishopsgate Street, Petty France, Bethlem Court and Lane, and Devonshire Square; besides which, there are little courts and alleys without number between Bishopsgate Street and Moorfields.

The public buildings in this ward are Leather-sellers' Hall, Gresham College, the churches of St. Botolph, Bishopsgate, St. Ethelburga, and St. Helen.

London Workhouse, for the poor of the City of London, also stands in this ward, just without Bishopsgate, being a long brick edifice four hundred feet in length, consisting of several work-rooms and lodging rooms for the vagrants and parish children brought thither, who are employed in spinning wool and flax, in sewing, knitting, or winding silk, or making their clothes or shoes, and are taught to write, read, and cast accounts. The grown vagrants brought here for a time only are employed in washing, beating hemp, and picking oakum, and have no more to keep them than they earn, unless they are sick; and the boys are put out apprentices to seafaring men or artificers, at a certain age, and in the meantime have their diet, clothes, physic, and other necessaries provided for them by the house, which is supported by private charities, by sums raised annually by the City, or by the labour of the children, which last article produces seven or eight hundred pounds per annum.

6. Broad Street Ward contains part of Threadneedle Street, Bartholomew Lane, part of Prince's Street, part of Lothbury, part of Throgmorton Street, great part of Broad Street, Winchester Street, Austinfriars, part of Wormwood Street, and part of London Wall Street, with the courts and lanes running into them.

The public buildings in this ward are Carpenters' Hall, Drapers' Hall, Merchant Taylors' Hall, the South Sea House, the Pay Office, Allhallows on the Wall, St. Peter's Poor, the Dutch Church, St. Martin's, St. Bennet's, St. Bartholomew's, St. Christopher's, and the French Church.

The most magnificent and beautiful edifice of the kind in this ward, and indeed in the City of London, is the South Sea House, lately erected at the north-east corner of Threadneedle Street, near Bishopsgate Street, and over against the church of St. Martin Outwich. It is built of stone and brick.

The several offices for transacting the business of this great company are admirably well disposed; and the great hall for sales is nowhere to be paralleled, either in its dimensions or ornaments, any more than the dining-room, galleries, and chambers above.

7. Cornhill Ward comprehends little more than the street of the same name, and some little lanes and alleys that fall into it, as Castle Alley, Sweeting's or Swithin's Alley, Freeman's Yard, part of Finch Lane, Weigh House Yard, Star Court, the north end of Birching Lane, St. Michael's Alley, Pope's Head Alley, and Exchange Alley.

Cornhill Street may, in many respects, be looked upon as the principal street of the City of London; for here almost all affairs relating to navigation and commerce are transacted; and here all the business relating to the great companies and the Bank are negotiated. This street also is situated near the centre of the City, and some say, upon the highest ground in it. It is spacious, and well built with lofty houses, four or five storeys high, inhabited by linendrapers and other considerable tradesmen, who deal by wholesale as well as retail, and adorned with the principal gate and front of the Royal Exchange. Here also it is said the metropolitan church was situated, when London was an archbishopric.

Exchange Alley, so denominated from its being situated on the south side of this street, over against the Royal Exchange, has long been famous for the great concourse of merchants and commanders of ships, and the bargains and contracts made there and in the two celebrated coffee-houses in it, which go under the respective names of "Jonathan's" and "Garraway's," where land, stocks, debentures, and merchandise, and everything that has an existence in Nature, is bought, sold, and transferred from one to another; and many things contracted for, that subsists only in the imagination of the parties.

The public buildings in this ward are, the Royal Exchange, and the churches of St. Peter and St. Michael.

The Royal Exchange is situated on the north side of Cornhill, about the middle of the street, forming an oblong open square, the inside whereof is a hundred and forty-four feet in length from east to west, and a hundred and seventeen in breadth from north to south; the area sixty-one square poles, on every side whereof is a noble piazza or cloister, consisting of twenty-eight columns and arches that support the galleries above.

The length of the building on the outside is two hundred and three feet, the breadth a hundred and seventy-one, and the height fifty-six. On the front towards Cornhill also is a noble piazza, consisting of ten pillars; and another on the opposite side next Threadneedle Street, of as many; and in the middle of each a magnificent gate. Over the Cornhill gate is a beautiful tower, a hundred and seventy-eight feet high, furnished with twelve small bells for chimes; and underneath the piazzas are capacious cellars, which serve for warehouses.

The whole building is of Portland stone, rustic work; above the arches the inward piazza is an entablament, with fine enrichments; and on the cornice a range of pilasters, within entablature, and a spacious compass pediment in the middle of the corners of each of the four sides. Under the pediment on the north side are the king's arms; on the south those of the City; and on the east the arms of Sir Thomas Gresham. And under the pediment on the west side the arms of the Company of Mercers, with their respective enrichments. The intercolumns of the upper range are twenty-four niches, nineteen of which are filled with the statues of the kings and queens regent of England, standing erect with their robes and regalia, except that of King James II. and King George II., which are habited like the Caesars.

On the south side are seven niches, of which four are filled, *viz.*:-

1. The most easterly figure, which has this inscription in gold letters, Edvardus Primus Rex, Anno Dom. 1272. 2. Westward, Edvardus III. Rex, Anno Dom. 1329. 3. Henricus V. Rex, Anno Domini 1412. 4. Henricus VI. Rex, Anno Domini 1422.

On the west side five niches, four of which are filled, *viz.*:-

1. Under the most southerly figures is subscribed in gold letters, Edvardus IV. Rex, Anno Domini 1460. 2. Northward (the crown pendent over his head) Edvardus V. Rex, Anno Domini 1483. 3. Henricus VII. Rex, Anno Domini 1487. 4. Henricus VIII. Rex, Anno Domini 1508.

On the north side seven niches are filled, *viz.*:-

1. The most westerly, subscribed in golden characters, Edvardus VI. Rex, Anno Domini 1547. 2. Maria Regina, Anno Domini 1553. 3. Elizabetha Regina, Anno Domini 1558. 4. Is subscribed Serenissim & Potentissim' Princip' Jacobo Primo, Mag. Brit' Fran' & Hibern' Reg. Fid. Defensori, Societas Pannitonsorum posuit, A.D. 1684. 5. [Greek text which cannot be reproduced] Serenissimi & Religiosissimi Principis Caroli Primi, Angliae, Scotiae, Franciae Hiberniae Regis, Fidei Defensoris; Bis Martyris (in Corpore Effigie) Impiis Rebellium Manibus, ex hoc loco deturbata confracta, Anno Dom. 1647. Restituta hic demum collocata, Anno Dom. 1683. Gloria Martyrii qui te fregere Rebelles non potuere ipsum quem voluere Deum. 6. Carolus Secundus Rex, Anno Domini 1648. 7. Jacobus II. Rex, Anno Domini 1685.

On the east side five niches, one of which is vacant, the other filled, *viz.*:-

1. The most northerly contains two statues, *viz.*, of King William and Queen Mary, subscribed Gulielmus III. Rex, & Maria II. Regina, A.D. 1688. S. P. Q. Londin' Optim Principibus, P. C. 1695. 2. Anna Regina Dei Gratia Mag. Britan' Franciae & Hiberniae, 1701. 3. George I. inscribed Georgius D. G. Magnae Britan' Franciae & Hiberniae Rex, Anno Dom. 1714. S.P.Q.L. 4. Southerly the statue of King George II. in the habiliment of a Cæsar, wreathed on the head, and a battoon or truncheon in his hand, little differing from that of Charles II. in the centre of the area, only in looking northward; inscribed Georgius II. D. G. Mag. Brit. Fra. & Hib. Rex, Anno Dom. 1727. S.P.Q.L.

On the four sides of the piazza within the Exchange are twenty-eight niches, which are all vacant yet, except one near the north-west angle, where is the figure of Sir Thomas Gresham. The piazza itself is paved with black and white marble, and the court, or area, pitched with pebbles; in the middle whereof is the statue of King Charles II. in a Roman habit, with a battoon in his hand, erected on a marble pedestal, about eight feet high and looking southward; on which side of the pedestal, under an imperial crown, wings, trumpet of fame, sceptre and sword, palm branches, &c., are these words inscribed, *viz.*:-

Carolo II. Caesari Britannico, Patriae Patri, Regum Optimo Clementissimo Augustissimo, Generis Humani Deliciis, Utriusq; Fortunae Victori, Pacis Europae Arbitro, Marium Domino, ac Vindici Societatis Mercatorum Adventur' Angliae, quae per CCCC jam prope Annos Regia benignitate floret, Fidei Intemeratae & Gratitudinis aeternae hoc Testimonium venerabunda posuit, Anno Salutis Humanae 1684.

On the west side of the pedestal is neatly cut in relievo the figure of a Cupid reposing his right hand on a shield containing the arms of England and France quartered, and in his left hand a rose.

On the north side are the arms of Ireland on a shield, supported by a Cupid.

On the east side the arms of Scotland, with a Cupid holding a thistle all in relievo.

The inner piazza and court are divided into several stations, or walks, where the merchants of the respective nations, and those who have business with them, assemble distinctly; so that any merchant or commander of a vessel is readily found, if it be known to what country he trades. The several walks are described in the following ground-plot of the Exchange:-

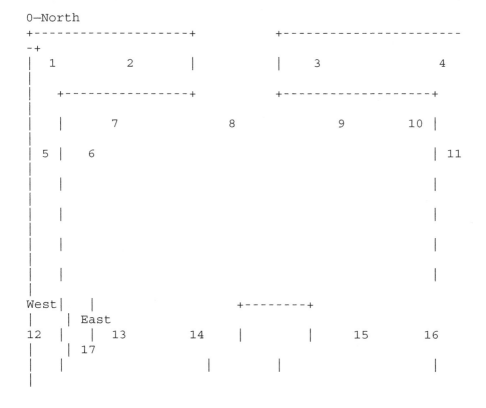

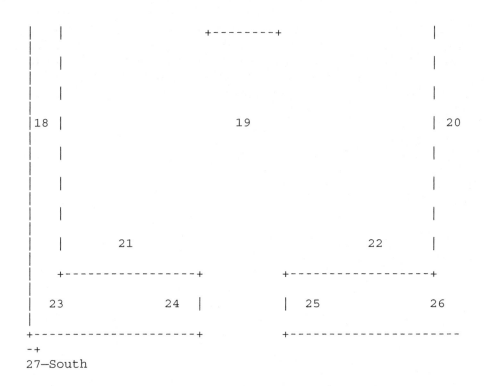

```
|   |                    + - - - - - - - - +                        |

|   |                                                               |

|   |                                                               |

| 18 |                            19                          | 20

|   |                                                               |

|   |                                                               |

|   |                                                               |

|   |      21                                          22          |

|   + - - - - - - - - - - - - - - - +        + - - - - - - - - - - - - - - - - - - +

|   23              24 |        | 25                  26

+ - - - - - - - - - - - - - - - - - - +        + - - - - - - - - - - - - - - - - - - - -
- +
```
27—South

0. Threadneedle Street 1. East Country Walk 2. Irish Walk 3. Scotch Walk 4. Dutch and Jewellers 5. Norway Walk 6. Silkmens Walk 7. Clothiers Walk 8. Hamburgh Walk 9. Salters Walk 10. Walk 11. American Walk 12. Castle Alley 13. Turkey Walk 14. Grocers and Druggists Walk 15. Brokers, &c of Stocks Walk 16. Italian Walk 17. Swithin's Alley 18. East India Walk 19. Canary Walk 20. Portugal Walk 21. Barbadoes Walk. 22. French Walk 23. Virginia Walk 24. Jamaica Walk. 25. Spanish Walk 26. Jews Walk 27. Cornhill

Near the south gate is a spacious staircase, and near the north gate another, that lead up to the galleries, on each side whereof are shops for milliners and other trades, to the number of near two hundred, which brought in a good revenue at first, nothing being thought fashionable that was not purchased there; but the milliners are now dispersed all over the town, and the shops in the Exchange almost deserted.

8. Langbourn Ward, so called of a bourne, or brook, that had its source in it, and run down Fenchurch Street, contains these principal streets: part of Lombard Street, part of Fenchurch Street, part of Lime Street, and part of Gracechurch Street, with part of the courts, lanes, and alleys in them, particularly White Hart Court, Exchange Alley, Sherbourne Lane, Abchurch Lane, St. Nicholas Lane, Mark Lane, Mincing Lane, Rood Lane, Cullum Court, Philpot Lane, and Braben Court.

The public buildings in this ward are, the Post Office, Ironmongers' Hall, Pewterers' Hall; the churches of Allhallows, Lombard Street, St. Edmund's, Lombard Street, St. Mary Woolnoth, St. Dionis Backchurch, and St. Allhallows Staining.

The Post Office is situated on the south side of Lombard Street, near Stocks Market. It was the dwelling-house of Sir Robert Vyner, in the reign of King Charles II. The principal entrance is out of Lombard Street, through a great gate and passage that leads into a handsome paved court, about which are the several offices for receiving and distributing letters, extremely well contrived.

Letters and packets are despatched from hence every Monday to France, Italy, Spain, Portugal, Flanders, Germany, Sweden, Denmark, Kent, and the Downs.

Every Tuesday to the United Netherlands, Germany, Sweden, Denmark, and to all parts of England, Scotland, and Ireland.

Every Wednesday to Kent only, and the Downs.

Every Thursday to France, Spain, Portugal, Italy, and all parts of England and Scotland.

Every Friday to the Austrian and United Netherlands, Germany, Sweden, Denmark, and to Kent and the Downs.

Every Saturday to all parts of England, Scotland, and Ireland.

The post goes also every day to those places where the Court resides, as also to the usual stations and rendezvous of His Majesty's fleet, as the Downs, Spithead, and to Tunbridge during the season for drinking waters, &c.

Letters and packets are received from all parts of England and Scotland, except Wales, every Monday, Wednesday, and Friday; from Wales every Monday and Friday; and from Kent and the Downs every day.

His Majesty keeps constantly, for the transport of the said letters and packets, in times of peace,

Between England and France, three packet-boats; Spain, one in a fortnight; Portugal, one ditto; Flanders, two packet-boats; Holland, three packet-boats; Ireland, three packet-boats.

And at Deal, two packet-boats for the Downs.

Not to mention the extraordinary packet-boats, in time of war with France and Spain, to the Leeward Islands, &c.

A letter containing a whole sheet of paper is conveyed eighty miles for 3d., and two sheets 6d. and an ounce of letters but 1s. And above eighty miles a single letter is 4d., a double letter 8d., and an ounce 1s. 4d.

9. Billingsgate Ward is bounded by Langbourn Ward towards the north, by Tower Street Ward on the east, by the River Thames on the south, and by Bridge Ward Within on the west. The principal streets and places in this ward are, Thames Street, Little East Cheap, Pudding Lane, Botolph Lane, Love Lane, St. Mary Hill, and Rood Lane.

The wharves, or quays, as they lie on the Thames side from east to west, are, Smart's Quay, Billings gate, Little Somer's Quay, Great Somer's Quay, Botolph Wharf, Cox's Quay, and Fresh Wharf which last is the next quay to the bridge; of which Billingsgate is much the most resorted to. It is a kind of square dock, or inlet, having quays on three sides of it, to which the vessels lie close while they are unloading. By a statute of the 10th and 11th of William III. it was enacted, "That Billingsgate should be a free market for fish every day in the week, except Sundays." That a fishing-vessel should pay no other toll or duty than the Act prescribes, viz., every salt-fish vessel, for groundage, 8d. per day, and 20d. per voyage; a lobster boat 2d. per day groundage, and 13d. the voyage; every dogger boat, or smack with sea-fish, 2d. per day groundage, and 13d. the voyage; every oyster vessel, 2d. per day groundage, and a halfpenny per bushel metage. And that it should be lawful for any person who should buy fish in the said market to sell the same in any other market or place in London, or elsewhere, by retail." And because the fishmongers used to buy up great part of the fish at Billingsgate, and then divide the same among themselves, in order to set an extravagant price upon them, it was enacted, "That no person should buy, or cause to be bought, in the said market of Billingsgate, any quantity of fish, to be divided by lot among the fishmongers, or other persons, with an intent to sell them afterwards by retail; and that no fishmonger should buy any more than for his own use, on pain of 20 pounds." And by the 6th Annae it was enacted, "That no person should buy fish at Billingsgate to sell again in the same market; and that none but fishermen, their wives, or servants, should sell fish by retail at Billingsgate; and that none should buy or sell fish there before the ringing of the market bell."

The public buildings in this ward are Butchers' Hall, and the churches of St. Mary Hill, St. Margaret Pattens, and St. George, in Botolph Lane.

10. Bridge Ward Within contains London Bridge, New Fish Street, Gracechurch Street as far as Fenchurch Street, Thames Street from Fish Street to the Old Swan, part of St. Martin's Lane, part of St. Michael's Lane, and part of Crooked Lane.

The public buildings in this ward are London Bridge, the Monument, Fishmongers' Hall, and the churches of St. Magnus and St Bennet, Gracechurch Street.

The Monument stands on the west side of Fish Street Hill, a little to the northward of the bridge, and was erected by the legislative authority, in memory of the Fire, anno 1666, and was designed by Sir Christopher Wren. It has a fluted column, 202 feet high from the ground; the greatest diameter of the shaft 15 feet, and the plinth, or lowest part of the pedestal, 28 feet square, and 40 feet high; the whole being of Portland stone, except the staircase within, which is of black marble, containing 345 steps, ten inches and a half broad, and six inches deep; and a balcony on the outside 32 feet from the top, on which is a gilded flame. The front of the pedestal, towards the west, contains a representation of the Fire, and the resurrection of the present city out of the ruins of the former.

11. Candlewick or Cannon Street Ward contains part of Great East Cheap, part of Candlewick, now called Cannon Street, part of Abchurch Lane, St. Nicholas Lane, St. Clement's Lane, St. Michael's Lane, Crooked Lane, St. Martin's Lane, St. Lawrence Poultney Lane, with the courts and alleys that fall into them.

In Cannon Street is that remarkable stone called London Stone, which has remained fixed in the ground many hundred years, but for what end is uncertain, though supposed by some to be the place from whence the Romans began to compute the number of miles anciently to any part of the kingdom.

12. Walbrook Ward contains the best part of Walbrook, part of Bucklersbury, the east end of Budge Row, the north end of Dowgate, part of Cannon Street, most of Swithin's Lane, most of Bearbinder Lane, part of Bush Lane, part of Suffolk Lane, part of Green Lattice Lane, and part of Abchurch Lane, with several courts and lanes that fall into them.

Stocks Market consists of a pretty large square, having Cornhill and Lombard Street on the north-east, the Poultry on the north-west, and Walbrook on the south-east. Before the Fire it was a market chiefly for fish and flesh, and afterwards for fruit and garden stuff.

In this market Sir Robert Vyner, Bart. and Alderman, erected a marble equestrian statue of King Charles II., standing on a pedestal eighteen feet high, and trampling on his enemies.

The public buildings in this ward are Salters' Hall, the churches of St. Swithin and St. Stephen, Walbrook.

13. Dowgate, or Dowgate Ward, so called from the principal street, which has a steep descent or fall into the Thames, contains part of Thames Street, part of St. Lawrence-Poultney Hill, part of Duxford Lane, part of Suffolk Lane, part of Bush Lane, part of Dowgate Hill, Checquer Yard, Elbow Lane, and Cloak Lane; and the southward of Thames Street, Old Swan Lane, Cole Harbour, Allhallows Lane, Campion Lane, Friars Lane, Cozens Lane, Dowgate Dock, and the Steel Yard.

The public buildings in this ward are Tallow-chandlers' Hall, Skinners' Hall, Innholders' Hall, Plumbers' Hall, Joiners' Hall, Watermen's Hall, and the church of Allhallows the Great.

14. Vintry Ward (which was so called from the wine merchants who landed and sold their wines here) contains part of Thames Street, New Queen Street, Garlick Hill, College Hill, and St. Thomas Apostles.

The public buildings in this ward are Vintners' Hall, Cutlers' Hall, the churches of St. Michael Royal and St. James, Garlick Hill.

Vintners' Hall is situated on the south side of Thames Street, between Queen Street and Garlick Hill, being built on three sides of a quadrangle fronting the street. The rooms are large, finely wainscoted and carved, particularly the magnificent screen at the east end of the great hall, which is adorned with two columns, their entablature and pediment; and on acroters are placed the figure of Bacchus between several Fames, with other embellishments; and they have a garden backwards towards the Thames.

15. Cordwainers' Street Ward, so called from the cordwainers (shoemakers), curriers, and other dealers in leather, that inhabited that part of the town anciently, includes Bow Lane, New Queen Street, Budge Row, Tower Royal Street, Little St. Thomas Apostle's, Pancras Lane, a small part of Watling Street, a little part of Basing Lane, and St. Sythe's Lane.

The public buildings in this ward are the church of St. Anthony, St. Mary Aldermary, and St. Mary-le-Bow.

16. Cheap Ward. The principal streets and places in this ward are Cheapside, the Poultry, part of Honey Lane Market, part of the Old Jewry, part of Bucklersbury, part of Pancras Lane, part of Queen Street, all Ironmonger Lane, King Street, and St. Lawrence Lane, and part of Cateaton Street, part of Bow Lane, and all Guildhall.

The public buildings in this ward are, Guildhall, Mercers' Chapel and Hall, Grocers' Hall, the Poultry Compter, the churches of St. Mildred, Poultry, and St. Lawrence Jewry.

Guildhall, the town house of this great City, stands at the north end of King Street, and is a large handsome structure, built with stone, anno 1666, the old hall having been destroyed by the Fire in 1666. By a large portico on the south side we enter the principal room, properly called the hall, being 153 feet in length, 48 in breadth, and 55 in height. On the right hand, at the upper end, is the ancient court of the hustings; at the other end of the hall opposite to it are the Sheriff's Courts. The roof of the inside is flat, divided into panels; the walls on the north and south sides adorned with four demy pillars of the Gothic order, painted white, and veined with blue, the capitals gilt with gold, and the arms finely depicted in their proper colour, *viz.*, at the east the arms of St. Edward the Confessor, and of the Kings of England the shield and cross of St. George. At the west end the arms of the Confessor, those of England and France quarterly, and the arms of England. On the fourteen demy pillars (above the capital) are the king's arms, the arms of London, and the arms of the twelve companies. At the east end are the King's arms carved between the portraits of the late Queen, at the foot of an arabathram, under a rich canopy northward, and those of King William and Queen Mary southward, painted at full length. The inter-columns are painted in imitation of porphyry, and embellished with the portraitures, painted in full proportion, of eighteen judges, which were there put up by the City, in gratitude for their signal service done in determining differences between landlord and tenant (without the expense of lawsuits) in rebuilding this City, pursuant to an Act of Parliament, after the Fire, in 1666.

Those on the south side are, Sir Heneage Finch, Sir Orlando Bridgeman, Sir Matthew Hale, Sir Richard Rainsford, Sir Edward Turner, Sir Thomas Tyrrel, Sir John Archer, Sir William Morton.

On the north side are, Sir Robert Atkins, Sir John Vaughan, Sir Francis North, Sir Thomas Twisden, Sir Christopher Turner, Sir William Wild, Sir Hugh Windham.

At the west end, Sir William Ellis, Sir Edward Thurland, Sir Timothy Littleton.

And in the Lord Mayor's Court (which is adorned with fleak stone and other painting and gilding, and also the figures of the four cardinal virtues) are the portraits of Sir Samuel Brown, Sir John Kelynge, Sir Edward Atkins, and Sir William Windham, all (as those above) painted in full proportion in their scarlet robes as judges.

The late Queen Anne, in December, 1706, gave the City 26 standards, and 63 colours, to be put up in this hall, that were taken from the French and Bavarians at the battle of Ramillies the preceding summer; but there was found room only for 46 colours, 19 standards, and the trophy of a kettle-drum of the Elector of Bavaria's. The colours over the Queen's picture are most esteemed, on account of their being taken from the first battalion of French guards.

From the hall we ascend by nine stone steps to the Mayor's Court, Council Chamber, and the rest of the apartments of the house, which, notwithstanding it may not be equal to the grandeur of the City, is very well adapted to the ends it was designed for, namely, for holding the City courts, for the election of sheriffs and other officers, and for the entertainment of princes, ministers of State, and foreign ambassadors, on their grand festivals.

17. Coleman Street Ward. The principal streets in this ward are the Old Jewry, part of Lothbury, Coleman Street, part of London Wall, and all the lower part of Moorfields without the walls.

The public buildings are Bethlem or Bedlam Hospital, Founders' Hall, Armourers' Hall, the churches of St. Olave Jewry, St. Margaret, Lothbury, and St. Stephen, Coleman Street.

New Bethlem, or Bedlam, is situated at the south end of Moorfields, just without the wall, the ground being formerly part of the town ditch, and granted by the City to the governors of the hospital of Old Bethlem, which had been appropriated for the reception of lunatics, but was found too strait to contain the people brought thither, and the building in a decaying condition.

The present edifice, called New Bedlam, was begun to be erected anno 1675, and finished the following year. It is built of brick and stone; the wings at each end, and the portico, being each of them adorned with four pilasters, entablature and circular pediment of the Corinthian order. Under the pediment are the King's arms, enriched with festoons; and between the portico and each of the said wings is a triangular pediment, with the arms of the City; and on a pediment over the gate the figures of two lunatics, exquisitely carved. The front of this magnificent hospital is reported to represent the Escurial in Spain, and in some respects exceeds every palace in or about London, being 528 feet in length, and regularly built. The inside, it is true, is not answerable to the grand appearance it makes without, being but 30 feet broad, and consisting chiefly of a long gallery in each of the two storeys that runs from one end of the house to the other; on the south side whereof are little cells, wherein the patients have their lodgings, and on the north the windows that give light to the galleries, which are divided in the middle by a handsome iron gate, to keep the men and women asunder.

In order to procure a person to be admitted into the hospital, a petition must be preferred to a committee of the governors, who sit at Bedlam seven at a time weekly, which must be signed by the churchwardens, or other reputable persons of the parish the lunatic belongs to, and also recommended to the said committee by one of the governors; and this being approved by the president and governors, and entered in a book, upon a vacancy (in their turn) an order is granted for their being received into the house, where the said lunatic is accommodated with a room, proper physic and diet, gratis. The diet is very good and wholesome, being commonly boiled beef, mutton, or veal, and broth, with bread, for dinners on Sundays, Tuesdays, and Thursdays, the other days bread, cheese, and butter, or on Saturdays pease-pottage, rice-milk, furmity, or other pottage, and for supper they have usually broth or milk pottage, always with bread. And there is farther care taken, that some of the committee go on a Saturday weekly to the said hospital to see the provisions weighed, and that the same be good and rightly expended.

18. Basinghall, or Bassishaw Ward, consisteth only of Basinghall Street, and a small part of the street along London Wall.

The public buildings of this ward are Blackwell Hall, Masons' Hall, Weavers' Hall, Coopers' Hall, Girdlers' Hall, and St. Michael Bassishaw Church.

Blackwell Hall is situated between Basinghall Street on the east, and Guildhall Yard on the west, being formerly called Bakewell Hall, from the family of the Bakewells, whose mansion-house stood here anno 1315, which falling to the Crown, was purchased by the City of King Richard II., and converted into a warehouse and market for woollen manufactures; and by an act of common council anno 1516, it was appointed to be the only market for woollen manufactures sold in the City,

28

except baize, the profits being settled on Christ's Hospital, which arise from the lodging and pitching of the cloth in the respective warehouses, there being one assigned for the Devonshire cloths, and others for the Gloucester, Worcester, Kentish, Medley, Spanish cloths, and blankets. The profits also of the baize brought to Leadenhall are settled on the same hospital. These cloths pay a penny a week each for pitching, and a halfpenny a week resting; stockings and blankets pay by the pack, all which bring in a considerable revenue, being under the direction of the governors of Christ's Hospital. This hall was destroyed by the Fire, and rebuilt by Christ's Hospital, anno 1672. The doorcase on the front towards Guildhall is of stone, adorned with two columns, entablature, and pediment of the Doric order. In the pediment are the King's arms, and the arms of London under them, enriched with Cupids, &c.

19. Cripplegate Ward is usually divided into two parts, *viz.*, Cripplegate within the walls and Cripplegate without.

The principal streets and places in Cripplegate Ward within the walls are Milk Street, great part of Honey Lane Market, part of Cateaton Street, Lad Lane, Aldermanbury, Love Lane, Addle Street, London Wall Street, from Little Wood Street to the postern, Philip Lane, most of Great Wood Street, Little Wood Street, part of Hart Street, Mugwell Street, part of Fell Street, part of Silver Street, the east part of Maiden Lane, and some few houses in Cheapside to the eastward of Wood Street.

The principal streets and places in Cripplegate Ward Without are Fore Street, and the Postern Street heading to Moorfields, Back Street in Little Moorfields, Moor Lane, Grub Street, the south part to the posts and chain, the fourth part of Whitecross Street as far as the posts and chain, part of Redcross Street, Beach Lane, the south part of Golden Lane as far as the posts and chain, the east part of Golden Lane, the east part of Jewin Street, Bridgewater Square, Brackley Street, Bridgewater Street, Silver Street, and Litton Street.

The public buildings in this ward are Sion College, Barber-Surgeons' Hall, Plasterers' Hall, Brewers' Hall, Curriers' Hall, the churches of St. Mary Aldermanbury, St. Alphege, St. Alban, Wood Street, and St. Giles, Cripplegate.

Sion College is situated against London Wall, a little to the eastward of Cripplegate, where anciently stood a nunnery, and afterwards a hospital founded for a hundred blind men, anno 1320, by W. Elsing, mercer, and called Elsing's Spittal: he afterwards founded here a priory for canons regular, which being surrendered to King Henry VIII. anno 1530, it was purchased by Dr. Thomas White, residentiary of St. Paul's, and vicar of St. Dunstan's in the West, for the use of the London clergy, who were incorporated by King Charles I., anno 1631, by the name of the president and fellows of Sion College, for the glory of God, the good of His Church, redress of inconveniences, and maintaining of truth in doctrine, and love in conversation with one another, pursuant to the donor's will; which college is governed by the president, two deans and four assistants, who are yearly elected out of the London clergy, on the third Tuesday after Easter; but none of them reside there, the whole being left to the care of the librarian. The great gate against London Wall is adorned with two columns, their entablature and pitched pediment of the Tuscan order, whereon is this inscription in gold letters:-

Collegium Sionis a Thoma White, S. T. P. Fundatum Anno Christi 1631, in Usum Clerici Lond. Bibliotheca a Johanne Simpson, S. T. B. Extracta, a diversis Benefactor, Libris locupletata, & in posterum locupletanda. Vade & fac similiter.

The college consists of a handsome hall, the president's lodgings, chambers for students, and a well-disposed library, one hundred and twenty feet in length, and thirty in breadth, which is at this day very well replenished with books, notwithstanding both library and college were burnt down anno 1666. It was rebuilt and furnished by contributions from the London clergy and their friends. The library is kept in exact order, and there are all imaginable conveniences for those who desire to consult their books.

20. Aldersgate Ward. The principal streets and places in this ward are, Foster Lane, Maiden Lane, Noble Street, St. Martin's-le-Grand, Dean's Court, Round Court, Angel Street, Bull-and-Mouth Street, St. Anne's Lane, Aldersgate Street, Goswell Street, Barbican, Long Lane, and Little Britain.

St. Martin's-le-Grand was anciently a magnificent college, founded by Jugelricus and Edwardus his brother, anno 1056, and confirmed by William the Conqueror, by his charter, dated anno 1068, in the second year of his reign, who also gave all the moorlands without Cripplegate to this college, exempting the dean and canons from the jurisdiction of the bishop, and from all legal services, granting them soc and sac, toll and theam, with all liberties and franchises that any church in the kingdom enjoyed.

This college was surrendered to King Edward VI. in the second year of his reign, anno 1548, and the same year the church pulled down, and the ground leased out to persons to build upon, being highly valued on account of the privileges annexed to it, for it still remains a separate jurisdiction. The sheriffs and magistrates of London have no authority in this liberty, but it is esteemed part of Westminster, and subject only to the dean and chapter of that abbey.

The public buildings in this ward are, Goldsmiths' Hall, Coachmakers' Hall, London House, Thanet House, Cooks' Hall, the church of St. Anne within Aldersgate, St. Leonard, Foster Lane, and St. Botolph, Aldersgate.

21. Farringdon Ward within the walls, so called to distinguish it from Farringdon Ward without, was anciently but one ward, and governed by one alderman, receiving its name of William Farendon, goldsmith, alderman thereof, and one of the sheriffs of London who purchased the aldermanry of John le Feure, 7 Edward I., anno 1279. It afterwards descended to Nicholas Farendon, son of the said William, who was four times mayor (and his heirs), from whence some infer that the aldermanries of London were formerly hereditary.

Farringdon Ward Within contains St. Paul's Churchyard, Ludgate Street, Blackfriars, the east side of Fleet Ditch, from Ludgate Street to the Thames, Creed Lane, Ave Mary Lane, Amen Corner, Paternoster Row, Newgate Street and Market, Greyfriars, part of Warwick Lane, Ivy Lane, part of Cheapside, part of Foster Lane, part of Wood Street, part of Friday Street, and part of the Old Change, with several courts and alleys falling into them.

The public buildings in this ward are, the Cathedral of St. Paul, St. Paul's School, the King's Printing House, the Scotch Hall, Apothecaries' Hall, Stationers' Hall, the College of Physicians, Butchers' Hall, Saddlers' Hall, Embroiderers' Hall, the church of St. Martin Ludgate, Christ's Church and Hospital, the church of St. Matthew, Friday Street, St. Austin's Church, the church of St Vedast, and the Chapter House.

Austin the monk was sent to England by Pope Gregory the Great, to endeavour the conversion of the Saxons, about the year 596, and being favourably received by Ethelbert, then King of Kent, who soon after became his proselyte, was by the authority of the Roman see constituted Archbishop of Canterbury, the capital of King Ethelbert's dominions. The archbishop being thus established in Kent, sent his missionaries into other parts of England, making Melitus, one of his assistants, Bishop of London; and King Ethelbert, to encourage that city to embrace Christianity, it is said, founded the Cathedral of St. Paul about the year 604.

This Cathedral stands upon an eminence in the middle of the town, disengaged from all other buildings, so that its beauties may be viewed on every side; whereas we see only one front of St. Peter's at Rome, the palace of the Vatican, and other buildings contiguous to it, rendering the rest invisible; and though the riches and furniture of the several chapels in St. Peter's are the admiration of all that view them, yet they spoil the prospect of the fabric. If we regard only the building, divested of the rich materials and furniture which hide the beauties of the structure, St. Paul's, in the opinion of many travellers, makes a better appearance than St. Peter's: nor does the white Portland stone, of which St. Paul's is built, at all give place to the marble St. Peter's is lined or incrusted with; for the numerous lamps and candles that are burnt before the altars at St. Peter's so blacken and tarnish the marble, that it is not easy to distinguish it from common stone. ·

As to the outside of St. Paul's, it is adorned by two ranges of pilasters, one above the other; the lower consist of 120 pilasters at least, with their entablature of the Corinthian order, and the upper of as many with entablament of the Composite order, besides twenty columns at the west and four at the east end, and those of the porticoes and spaces between the arches of the windows; and the architrave of the lower order, &c., are filled with great variety of curious enrichments, consisting of cherubims, festoons, volutas, fruit, leaves, car-touches, ensigns of fame, as swords and trumpets in saltier crosses, with chaplets of laurel, also books displayed, bishops' caps, the dean's arms, and, at the east end, the cypher of W.R. within a garter, on which are the words Honi soit qui mal y pense, and this within a fine compartment of palm-branches, and placed under an imperial crown, &c., all finely carved in stone.

The intercolumns of the lower range of pilasters are thirty-three ornamental windows and six niches, and of the upper range thirty-seven windows and about thirty niches, many whereof are adorned with columns, entablature, and pediments; and at the east end is a sweep, or circular space, adorned with columns and pilasters, and enriched with festoons, fruit, incense-pots, &c., and at the upper part is a window between four pieddroits and a single cornice, and those between two large cartouches.

The ascent to the north portico is by twelve steps of black marble; the dome of the portico is supported and adorned with six very spacious columns (forty-eight inches diameter) of the Corinthian order. Above the doorcase is a large urn, with festoons, &c. Over this (belonging to the upper range of pilasters) is a spacious pediment, where are the king's arms with the regalia, supported by two angels, with each a palm-branch in their hands, under whose feet appear the figures of the lion and unicorn.

You ascend to the fourth portico (the ground here being low) by twenty-five steps. It is in all other respects like the north, and above this a pediment, as the other, belonging to the upper order, where is a proper emblem of this incomparable structure, raised, as it were, out of the ruins of the old church, *viz.*, a phoenix, with her wings expanded, in flames, under which is the word *resurgam* insculped in capital characters.

The west portico is adorned and supported with twelve columns below and eight above, fluted, of the respective orders as the two ranges, the twelve lower adorned with architrave, marble frieze, and a cornice, and the eight upper with an entablature and a spacious triangular pediment, where the history of St. Paul's conversion is represented, with the rays of a glory and the figures of several men and horses boldly carved in relievo by Mr. Bird. The doorcase is white marble, and over the entrance is cut in relieve the history of St. Paul's preaching to the Bereans (as in Acts xvii. 2). It consists of a group of nine figures, besides that of St. Paul, with books, &c., lively represented by the same hand as "The Conversion."

On the south side of the church, near the west end, is a forum or portal, the doorcase being enriched with cartouches, volutas, and fruit, very excellently carved under a pediment, and opposite to this on the north side is the like doorcase. And, in brief, all the apertures are not only judiciously disposed for commodiousness, illumination of the fabric, &c., but are very ornamental.

At the west end is an acroteria of the figures of the twelve apostles, each about eleven feet high, with that of St. Paul on the angle of the pediment, and those of the four evangelists, two of each cumbent between as many angles on a circular pediment. Over the dials of the clock on the fronts of the two towers, also an entablature and circles of enrichment, where twelve stones compose the aperture, answering to the twelve hours.

The said towers are adorned with circular ranges of columns of the Corinthian order, with domes upon the upper part, and at the vertex of each a curious pineapple.

The choir has its roof supported with six spacious pillars, and the church with six more, besides which there are eight that support the cupola and two very spacious ones at the west end. All which pillars are adorned with pilasters of the Corinthian and Composite orders, and also with columns fronting the cross-aisle, or ambulatory, between the consistory and morning prayer chapel, which have each a very beautiful screen of curious wainscot, and adorned each with twelve columns, their entablatures arched pediments, and the king's arms, enriched with cherubims, and each pediment between four vases, all curiously carved. These screens are fenced with ironwork, as is also the cornice at the west end of the church, and so eastward beyond the first arch.

The pillars of the church that support the roof are two ranges, with their entablature and beautiful arches, whereby the body of the church and choir are divided into three parts or aisles. The roof of each is adorned with arches and spacious peripheries of enrichments, as shields, leaves, chaplets, &c. (the spaces included being somewhat concave), admirably carved in stone; and there is a large cross aisle between the north and south porticoes, and two ambulatories, the one a little eastward, the other westward from the said cross-aisle, and running parallel therewith. The floor of the whole is paved with marble, but under the cupola and within the rail of the altar with fine porphyry, polished and laid in several geometrical figures.

The altar-piece is adorned with four noble fluted pilasters, finely painted and veined with gold, in imitation of lapis lazuli, with their entablature, where the enrichments, and also the capitals of the pilasters, are double gilt with gold. These intercolumns are twenty-one panels of figured crimson velvet, and above them six windows, *viz.*, in each intercolumniation seven panels and two windows, one above the other; at the greatest altitude above all which is a glory finely done. The aperture north and south into the choir are (ascending up three steps of black marble) by two iron folding-doors, being, as that under the organ-gallery, &c., exquisitely wrought into divers figures, spiral branches, and other flourishes. There are two others at the west end of the choir, the one opening into the south aisle, the other in the north, done by the celebrated artist in this way, M. Tijan.

And what contributes to the beauty of this choir are the galleries, the bishop's throne, Lord Mayor's seat, with the stalls, all which being contiguous, compose one vast body of carved work of the finest wainscot, constituting three sides of a quadrangle.

The cupola (within the church) appears erected and elevated on eight pillars of a large magnitude, adorned with pilasters, entablature, circular pediments, and arches of the Corinthian order, and each pillar enriched with a spacious festoon. Here are also as many alcoves fronted with curious ironwork, and over the arches, at a great height from the ground, is an entablature, and on the cornice an ambulatory, fronted or fenced in with handsome ironwork, extending round the inside of the cupola, above which is a range of thirty-two pilasters of the Corinthian order, where every fourth intercolumn is adorned with a niche and some enrichments; and it said that in every foot of altitude the diameter of this decreaseth one inch.

On the outside of the dome, about twenty feet above the outer roof of the church, is a range of thirty-two columns, with niches of the same altitude, and directly counter to those aforesaid within the cupola. To these columns there is entablament, and above that a gallery with acroteria, where are placed very spacious and ornamental vases all round the cupola. At twelve feet above the tops of these vases (which space is adorned with pilasters and entablament, and the intercolumns are windows) the diameter is taken in (as appears outwardly) five feet, and two feet higher it decreases five feet, and a foot above that it is still five feet less, where the dome outwardly begins to arch, which arches meet about fifty-two feet higher in perpendicular altitude, on the vertex of which dome is a neat balcony, and above this a large and beautiful lantern, adorned with columns of the Corinthian order, with a ball and cross at the top.

Christ's Hospital is situated between Newgate Street and St. Bartholomew's Hospital in Smithfield. Here, as has been observed already, was anciently a monastery of grey friars, founded about the year 1325, which, upon the dissolution of monasteries, was surrendered to King Henry VIII., anno 1538, who, in the last year of his reign, transferred it to the City of London for the use of the poor. King Edward VI. endowed this hospital—together with those of Bridewell and St. Thomas's Hospital in Southwark—with large revenues, of which the City were made trustees, and incorporated by the name of the mayor, commonalty, and citizens of the City of London, governors of the possessions, revenues, and goods of the hospitals of Christ, Bridewell, and St. Thomas the Apostle, to whom the king granted 3,266 pounds 13s. 4d. per annum.

It was opened in the year 1552, in the month of November, and a good writing-school was added to this foundation in the year 1694 by Sir John More, Kt., and alderman.

The children admitted into this hospital are presented every year by the Lord Mayor and aldermen and the other governors in their turns, a list of whom is printed yearly and set up at the counting-house, and a letter is sent to each of the said governors, some days before the admission, reminding him of the day of choosing, and how those he presents should be qualified, wherein is enclosed a blank certificate from the minister and churchwardens, a blank petition to the president and governors, and a paper of the rules and qualifications of the child to be presented. Upon this the governor, having made choice of a child to present, the friends of the said child come to the counting-house on the admission-day, bringing the said petition and certificates, rules, and letter along with him, and on the back side of the said petition the governor who presents endorseth words to this effect.

"I present the child mentioned in the certificate on the other side, and believe the same to be a true certificate.

"Witness my hand . . . the day . . . of 17." Which the said governor signeth, and the child is admitted.

The said rules and qualifications are as follows:

1. That no child be taken in but such as are the children of freemen of London.

2. That none be taken in under seven years old.

3. That none be taken in but orphans, wanting either father or mother, or both.

4. That no foundlings, or that are maintained at the parish charge, be taken in.

5. That none who are lame, crooked, or deformed, or that have the evil, rupture, or any infectious disease, be taken in.

6. That none be admitted but such as are without any probable means of being provided for otherways; nor without a due certificate from the minister, churchwardens, and three or four of the principal inhabitants of the parish whence any children come, certifying the poverty and inability of the parent to maintain such children, and the true age of the said child, and engaging to discharge the hospital of them before or after the age of fifteen years if a boy, or fourteen years if a girl, which shall be left to the governor's pleasure to do; so that it shall be wholly in the power of the hospital to dispose of such child, or return them to the parent or parish, as to the hospital shall seem good.

7. That no child be admitted that hath a brother or sister in the hospital already.

8. To the end that no children be admitted contrary to the rules abovesaid, when the general court shall direct the taking in of any children, they shall (before taken in) be presented to a committee, consisting of the president, treasurer, or the almoners, renters, scrutineers, and auditors, and all other governors to be summoned at the first time, and so to adjourn from time to time: and that they, or any thirteen or more of them, whereof the president or treasurer for the time being to be one, shall strictly examine touching the age, birth, and quality of such children, and of the truth of the said certificates; and when such committee shall find cause, they shall forbid or suspend the taking in of any child, until they receive full satisfaction that such child or children are duly qualified according to the rules abovesaid.

And that such children as may be presented to be admitted in pursuance of the will of any benefactor, shall be examined by the said committee, who are to take care that such children be qualified according to the wills of the donors or benefactors (as near as may consist with such wills) agreeing to the qualifications above.

The Lord Mayor and Court of Aldermen present each their child yearly, but the rest of the governors only in their turns, which may happen once in three or four years.

No child is continued in after fifteen years of age, except the mathematical scholars, who are sometimes in till they are eighteen, and who, at the beginning of the seventh year of their service as mariners are at His Majesty's disposal; and of these children there is an account printed yearly, and presented to the king the 1st of January, setting forth, (1) each boy's name; (2) the month and year when they were bound out; (3) their age; (4) the names of their masters; (5) the names of the ships whereof they are commanders; (6) what country trade they are in; (7) the month and year when they will be at His Majesty's disposal. Also an account of the forty children annually enjoying the benefit of this mathematical foundation, &c., setting forth their names and age.

The governors, besides the Lord Mayor and aldermen, are many, and commonly persons that have been masters or wardens of their companies, or men of estates, from whom there is some expectation of additional charities. Out of these one is made president, who is usually some ancient alderman that hath passed the chair; another is appointed treasurer, to whom the care of the house and of the revenues are committed, who is therefore usually resident, and has a good house within the limits of the hospital. There are two governors also, who are called almoners, whose business it is to buy provisions for the house and send them in, who are attended by the steward.

The children are dieted in the following manner: They have every morning for their breakfast bread and beer, at half an hour past six in the morning in the summer time, and at half an hour past seven in the winter. On Sundays they have boiled beef and broth for their dinners, and for their suppers legs and shoulders of mutton. On Tuesdays and Thursdays they have the same dinners as on Sundays, that is, boiled beef and broth; on the other days no flesh meat, but on Mondays milk-porridge, on Wednesdays furmity, on Fridays old pease and pottage, on Saturdays water-gruel. They have roast beef about twelve days in the year by the kindness of several benefactors, who have left, some 3 pounds, some 50s. per annum, for that end. Their supper is bread and cheese, or butter for those who cannot eat cheese; only Wednesdays and Fridays they heave pudding-pies for supper.

The diet of these children seems to be exceeding mean and sparing; and I have heard some of their friends say that it would not be easy for them to subsist upon it without their assistance. However, it is observed they are very healthful; that out of eleven or twelve hundred there are scarce ever found twelve in the sick ward; and that in one year, when there were upwards of eleven hundred in this hospital, there were not more than fifteen of them died. Besides, their living in this thrifty parsimonious manner, makes them better capable of shifting for themselves when they come out into the world.

As to the education of these orphans, here is a grammar-school, a writing-school, a mathematical-school, and a drawing-school.

As to grammar and writing, they have all of them the benefit of these schools without distinction; but the others are for such lads as are intended for the sea-service.

The first mathematical school was founded by King Charles II., anno domini 1673. His Majesty gave 7,000 pounds towards building and furnishing this school, and settled a revenue of 370 pounds per annum upon it for ever; and there has been since another mathematical school erected here, which is maintained out of the revenues of the hospital, as is likewise the drawing-school.

This hospital is built about a large quadrangle, with a cloister or piazza on the inside of it, which is said to be part of the monastery of the Grey Friars; but most part of the house has been rebuilt since the Fire, and consists of a large hall, and the several schools and dormitories for the children; besides which there is a fine house at Hertford, and another at Ware, twenty miles from London, whither the youngest orphans are usually sent, and taught to read, before they are fixed at London.

The College of Physicians is situated on the west side of Warwick Lane. It is a beautiful and magnificent edifice, built by the society anno 1682, their former college in Amen Corner having been destroyed by the Fire. It is built of brick and stone, having a fine frontispiece, with a handsome doorcase, within which is a lofty cupola erected on strong pillars, on the top whereof is a large pyramid, and on its vertex a crown and gilded ball. Passing under the cupola we come into a quadrangular court, the opposite side whereof is adorned with eight pilasters below and eight above, with their entablature and a triangular pediment; over the doorcase is the figure of King Charles II. placed in a niche and between the door and the lower architrave the following inscription, *viz.*:-

VTRIVSQVE FORTVNAE *exemplar* INGENS ADVERSIS REBVS DEVM PROBAVIT PROSPERIS SEIPSVM COLLEGIJ HVJUSCE, 1682.

The apartments within consist of a hall, where advice is given to the poor gratis; a committee-room, a library, another great hall, where the doctors meet once a quarter, which is beautifully wainscoted, carved, and adorned with fretwork. Here are the pictures of Dr. Harvey, who first discovered the circulation of the blood, and other benefactors, and northward from this, over the library, is the censor's room.

The theatre under the cupola at the entrance is furnished with six degrees of circular wainscot seats, one above the other, and in the pit is a table and three seats, one for the president, a second for the operator, and a third for the lecturer; and here the anatomy lectures are performed. In the preparing room are thirteen tables of the muscles in a human body, each muscle in its proper position.

This society is a body-corporate for the practice of physic within London, and several miles about it. The president and censors are chosen annually at Michaelmas. None can practise physic, though they have taken their degrees, without their license, within the limits aforesaid; and they have a power to search all apothecaries' shops, and to destroy unwholesome medicines.

By the charter of King Charles II. this college was to consist of a president, four censors, ten elects, and twenty-six fellows; the censors to be chosen out of the fellows, and the president out of the elects.

By the charter granted by King James II., the number of fellows was enlarged, but not to exceed eighty, and none but those who had taken the degree of doctors in the British or foreign universities were qualified to be admitted members of this college.

The fellows meet four times every year, *viz.*, on the Monday after every quarter-day, and two of them meet twice a week, to give advice to the poor gratis. Here are also prepared medicines for the poor at moderate rates.

The president and four censors meet the first Friday in every month. The Lord Chancellor, chief justices, and chief baron, are constituted visitors of this corporation, whose privileges are established by several Acts of Parliament.

22. Bread Street Ward contains Bread Street, Friday Street, Distaff Lane, Basing Lane, part of the Old Change, part of Watling Street, part of Old Fish Street, and Trinity Lane, and part of Cheapside.

The only public buildings in this ward are the churches of Allhallows, Bread Street, and St. Mildred, Bread Street.

23. Queenhithe Ward includes part of Thames Street, Queenhithe, with the several lanes running southward to the Thames, Lambeth Hill, Fish Street Hill, Five Foot Lane, Little Trinity Lane, Bread Street Hill, Huggin Lane, with the south side of Great Trinity Lane, and part of Old Fish Streets.

Queenhithe lies to the westward of the Three Cranes, and is a harbour for barges, lighters, and other vessels, that bring meal, malt, and other provisions down the Thames; being a square inlet, with wharves on three sides of it, where the greatest market in England for meal, malt, &c., is held every day in the week, but chiefly on Mondays, Wednesdays, and Fridays. It received the name of Queenhithe, or harbour, from the duties anciently paid here to the Queens of England.

24. Baynard's Castle Ward contains Peter's Hill, Bennet's Hill, part of Thames Street, Paul's Wharf, Puddle Dock, Addle Hill, Knightrider Street, Carter Lane, Wardrobe Court, Paul's Chain, part of St. Paul's Churchyard, Dean's Court, part of Creed Lane, and part of Warwick Lane.

The public buildings in this ward are Doctors' Commons, the Heralds' Office, the churches of St. Bennet, Paul's Wharf, St. Andrew, Wardrobe, and St. Mary Magdalen, Old Fish Street.

38

Doctors' Commons, so called from the doctors of the civil law commoning together here as in a college, is situated on the west side of Bennet's Hill, and consists chiefly of one handsome square court. And here are held the Court of Admiralty, Court of Arches, and the Prerogative Court of the Archbishop of Canterbury. Near the Commons are the Prerogative Office and Faculty Office.

The Heralds' College or office is situated on the east side of Bennet's Hill, almost against Doctors' Commons. It is a spacious building, with a square court in the middle of it, on the north side whereof is the Court-room, where the Earl Marshal sits to hear causes lying in the court of honour concerning arms, achievements, titles of honour, &c.

25. The Ward of Farringdon Without includes Ludgate Hill, Fleet Street and Fleet Ditch, Sheer Lane, Bell Yard, Chancery Lane, Fetter Lane, Dean Street, New Street, Plough Yard, East and West Harding Street, Fleur-de-Lis Court, Crane Court, Red Lion Court, Johnson's Court, Dunstan's Court, Bolt Court, Hind Court, Wine Office Court, Shoe Lane, Racquet Court, Whitefriars, the Temples, Dorset or Salisbury Court, Dorset Street, Bridewell, the Old Bailey, Harp Alley, Holborn Hill, Castle Street or Yard, Cursitor Alley, Bartlett's Buildings, Holborn Bridge, Snow Hill, Pye Corner, Giltspur Street, Cow Lane, Cock Lane, Hosier Lane, Chick Lane, Smithfield, Long Lane, Bartholomew Close, Cloth Fair, and Duck Lane.

West Smithfield—or, rather, Smoothfield, according to Stow—is an open place, containing little more than three acres of ground at present, of an irregular figure, surrounded with buildings of various kinds. Here is held one of the greatest markets of oxen and sheep in Europe, as may easily be imagined when it appears to be the only market for live cattle in this great city, which is held on Mondays and Fridays. There is also a market for horses on Fridays; nor is there anywhere better riding-horses to be purchased, if the buyer has skill, though it must be confessed there is a great deal of jockeying and sharping used by the dealers in horseflesh. As for coach-horses, and those fit for troopers, they are usually purchased in the counties to the northward of the town. The famous fair on the feast of St. Bartholomew also is held in this place, which lasts three days, and, by the indulgence of the City magistrates, sometimes a fortnight. The first three days were heretofore assigned for business, as the sale of cattle, leather, &c., but now only for diversion, the players filling the area of the field with their booths, whither the young citizens resort in crowds.

The public buildings in this ward are Bridewell, Serjeants' Inn in Fleet Street, the Temple, the Six Clerks' Office, the Rolls, Serjeants' Inn in Chancery Lane, Clifford's Inn, the House of the Royal Society, Staple's Inn, Bernards' Inn, and Thavie's Inn, Justice Hall in the Old Bailey, and the Fleet Prison, with the churches of St. Bartholomew, and the hospital adjoining, the churches of St. Sepulchre, St. Andrew, Holborn, St. Bride's, and St. Dunstan's-in-the-West.

Bridewell is situated on the west side of Fleet Ditch, a little to the southward of Fleet Street, having two fronts, one to the east, and the other to the north, with a handsome great gate in each of them. It consists chiefly of two courts, the innermost being the largest and best built, four or five storeys high, on the south side whereof is a noble hall, adorned with the pictures of King Edward VI. and his Privy Council, King Charles, and King James II., Sir William Turner, Sir William Jeffreys, and other benefactors.

It was one of the palaces of the Kings of England till the reign of King Edward VI., who gave it to the City of London for the use of their poor, with lands of the value of 700 marks per annum, and bedding and furniture out of the Hospital of the Savoy, then suppressed.

Here are lodgings and several privileges for certain tradesmen, such as flax-dressers, tailors, shoemakers, &c., called art masters, who are allowed to take servants and apprentices to the number of about 140, who are clothed in blue vests at the charge of the house, their masters having the profit of their labour. These boys having served their times, have their freedom, and ten pound each given them towards carrying on their trades; and some of them have arrived to the honour of being governors of the house where they served.

This Hospital is at present under the direction of a president, and some hundreds of the most eminent and substantial citizens, with their inferior officers; and a court is held every Friday, where such vagrants and lewd people are ordered to receive correction in the sight of the Court, as are adjudged to deserve it.

Among the public buildings of this ward, that belonging to the Royal Society, situate at the north end of Two Crane Court, in Fleet Street, must not be omitted, though it be much more considerable on account of the learned members who assemble there, and the great advances that have been made by them of late years in natural philosophy, &c., than for the elegancy of the building.

During the grand rebellion, when the estates of the prime nobility and gentry were sequestered, and there was no court for them to resort to, the then powers encouraging only the maddest enthusiast, or the basest of the people, whom they looked upon as the fittest instruments to support their tyranny; some ingenious gentlemen, who had applied themselves chiefly to their studies, and abhorred the usurpation, proposed the erecting a society for the improvement of natural knowledge, which might be an innocent and inoffensive exercise to themselves in those troublesome times, and of lasting benefit to the nation. Their first meeting, it is said, were at the chambers of Mr. Wilkins (afterwards Bishop of Chester) in Wadham College, in Oxford, about the year 1650, and the members consisted of the Honourable Robert Boyle, Esq., Dr. Ward (afterwards Bishop of Salisbury), Sir Christopher Wren, Sir William Petty, Dr. Wallis, Dr. Goddard, and Dr. Hook (late Professor of Geometry), the above-named Bishop Wilkins, and others. In the year 1658 we find them assembling in Gresham College, in London, when were added to their number the Lord Brounker (their first president), Sir Robert Murray, John Evelyng, Esq., Sir George Ent, Dr. Croon, Henry Shingsby, Esq., and many others. And after the Restoration, his Majesty King Charles II. appeared so well pleased with the design, that he granted them a charter of incorporation, bearing date the

22nd of April, 15 Charles II., anno 1663, wherein he styled himself their founder, patron, and companion; and the society was from thenceforward to consist of a president, a council of twenty, and as many fellows as should be thought worthy of admission, with a treasurer, secretary, curators, and other officers.

When a gentleman desires to be admitted to the society, he procures one of the Corporation to recommend him as a person duly qualified, whereupon his name is entered in a book, and proper inquiries made concerning his merit and abilities; and if the gentleman is approved of, he appears in some following assembly, and subscribes a paper, wherein he promises that he will endeavour to promote the welfare of the society: and the president formally admits him by saying, "I do, by the authority and in the name of the Royal Society of London for improving of natural knowledge, admit you a member thereof." Whereupon the new fellow pays forty shillings to the treasurer, and two-and-fifty shillings per annum afterwards by quarterly payments, towards the charges of the experiments, the salaries of the officers of the house, &c.

Behind the house they have a repository, containing a collection of the productions of nature and art. They have also a well-chosen library, consisting of many thousand volumes, most of them relating to natural philosophy; and they publish from time to time the experiments made by them, of which there are a great number of volumes, called "Philosophical Transactions."

The Hospital of St. Bartholomew, on the south side of Smithfield, is contiguous to the church of Little St. Bartholomew. It was at first governed by a master, eight brethren, and four sisters, who had the care of the sick and infirm that were brought thither. King Henry VIII. endowed it with a yearly revenue of five hundred more yearly for the relief of one hundred infirm people. And since that time the hospital is so increased and enlarged, by the benefactions given to it, that it receives infirm people at present from all parts of England. In the year 1702 a beautiful frontispiece was erected towards Smithfield, adorned with pilasters, entablature, and pediment of the Ionic order, with the figure of the founder, King Henry VIII., in a niche, standing in full proportion; and the figures of two cripples on the pediment: but the most considerable improvements to the building were made in the year 1731, of the old buildings being pulled down, and a magnificent pile erected in the room of them about 150 feet in length, faced with a pure white stone, besides other additions now building.

There are two houses belonging to this hospital, the one in Kent Street, called the Lock, and the other at Kingsland, whither such unfortunate people as are afflicted with the French disease are sent and taken care of, that they may not prove offensive to the rest; for surely more miserable objects never were beheld, many of them having their noses and great part of their faces eaten off, and become so noisome frequently, that their stench cannot be borne, their very bones rotting while they remain alive.

This hospital is governed by the Lord Mayor and Aldermen, with about three hundred other substantial citizens and gentlemen of quality, who generally become benefactors; and from these and their friends the hospital has been able to subsist such numbers of infirm people, and to perform the surprising cures they have done; for the patients are duly attended by the best physicians and surgeons in London, and so well supplied with lodging and diet proper to their respective cases, that much fewer miscarry here, in proportion, than in the great hospital of invalids, and others the French so much boast of in Paris.

Those that have the immediate care of the hospital are, the president, the treasurer, the auditors of accounts, viewers of their revenues, overseers of the goods and utensils of the hospital, and the almoners, who buy in provisions and necessaries for the patients.

A committee, consisting of the treasurer, almoners, and some other of the governors, meet twice a week to inspect the government of the house, to discharge such persons as are cured, and to admit others.

26. Bridge Ward Without contains in chief the Borough, or Long Southwark, St. Margaret's Hill, Blackman Street, Stony Street, St. Thomas's Street, Counter Street, the Mint Street, Maiden Lane, the Bankside, Bandy-leg Walk, Bennet's Rents, George Street, Suffolk Street, Redcross Street, Whitecross Street, Worcester Street, Castle Street, Clink Street, Deadman's Place, New Rents, Gravel Lane, Dirty Lane, St. Olave's Street, Horselydown, Crucifix Lane, Five-foot Lane, Barnaby Street, Long Lane and Street.

The Bankside consists of certain houses so called from their lying on the south bank of the Thames to the westward of the bridge.

The public buildings in this ward are, St. Thomas's Church and Hospital, Guy's Hospital for Incurables, the church of St. Saviour, the church of St. Olave, and that of St. George, the Bridge House, the King's Bench Prison, the Marshalsea, and the Clink Prison, the Sessions House, Compter, and New Prison.

The Hospital of St. Thomas consists of four spacious courts, in the first of which are six wards for women. In the second stands the church, and another chapel, for the use of the hospital. Here also are the houses of the treasurer, hospitaller, steward, cook, and butler. In the third court are seven wards for men, with an apothecary's shop, store-rooms and laboratory. In the fourth court are two wards for women, with a surgery, hot and cold baths, &c. And in the year 1718 another magnificent building was erected by the governors, containing lodgings and conveniences for a hundred infirm persons. So that this hospital is capable of containing five hundred patients and upwards at one time; and there are between four and five thousand people annually cured and discharged out of it, many of them being allowed money to bear their charges to their respective dwellings.

But one of the greatest charities ever attempted by a private citizen was that of Thomas Guy, Esq., originally a bookseller of London, and afterwards a Member of Parliament for Tamworth, who, having acquired an immense fortune, founded a hospital for incurables, on a spot of ground adjoining to St. Thomas's Hospital, and saw the noble fabric in a good forwardness in his lifetime, assigning about two hundred thousand pounds towards the building, and endowing it, insomuch that it is computed there may be an ample provision for four hundred unhappy people, who shall be given over by physicians and surgeons as incurable. This gentleman died in December, 1724, having first made his will, and appointed trustees to see his pious design duly executed. He gave also several thousand pounds to Christ's Hospital, and a thousand pounds a piece to fifty of his poor relations; but the will being in print, I refer the reader to it for a more particular account of this noble charity.

The first church and hospital, dedicated to St. Thomas a Becket, was erected by the Prior of Bermondsey, so long since as the year 1013; but the hospital was refounded, and the revenues increased, anno 1215, by Peter de Rupibus, Bishop of Winchester, in whose diocese it was situated, continuing, however, to be held of the priors of Bermondsey till the year 1428, when the Abbot of Bermondsey relinquished his interest to the master of the hospital for a valuable consideration. In the year 1538 this hospital was surrendered to King Henry VIII., being then valued at 266 pounds 17s. 6d. per annum. And in the following reign, the City of London having purchased the buildings of the Crown, continued them a hospital for sick and wounded people; and King Edward VI. granted them some of the revenues of the dissolved hospitals and monasteries towards maintaining it: but these were inconsiderable in comparison of the large and numerous benefactions that have since been bestowed upon it by the Lord Mayor, aldermen, and other wealthy citizens and men of quality, governors of it, who are seldom fewer than two or three hundred, every one of them looking upon themselves to be under some obligation of making an addition to the revenues of the hospital they have the direction of. A committee of the governors sit every Thursday, to consider what patients are fit to be discharged, and to admit others.

The government of the City of London, it is observed, resembles that of the kingdom in general; the Lord Mayor is compared to the king, the aldermen to the nobility or upper house, and the common councilmen to the commons of England.

This assembly, consisting of the Lord Mayor, aldermen, and common councilmen, has obtained the name of The Common Council, and has a power, by their charters, of making such bye-laws and statutes as are obligatory to the citizens. It is called and adjourned by the Lord Mayor at pleasure, and out of it are formed several committees, *viz.*—1. A committee of six aldermen and twelve commoners for letting the City lands, which usually meets every Wednesday at Guildhall for that end. 2. A committee of four aldermen and eight commoners for letting the lands and tenements given by Sir Thomas Gresham, who meets at Mercers' Hall on a summons from the Lord Mayor. 3. Commissioners of Sewers and Pavements, elected annually. And, 4. A governor, deputy-governor and assistants, for the management of City lands in the province of Ulster in Ireland.

The other principal courts in the City are, 1. The Court of Aldermen. 2. The Court of Hustings. 3. The Lord Mayor's Court. 4. The Sheriff's Court. 5. The Chamberlain's Court. 6. The Court of the City Orphans. 7. The Court of Conscience. 8. The Courts of Wardmote. And, 9. The Courts of Hallmote.

Besides which, there is a Court of Oyer and Terminer and Jail Delivery, held eight times a year at Justice Hall in the Old Bailey, for the trial of criminals.

1. In the Lord Mayor and Court of Aldermen is lodged the executive power in a great measure, and by these most of the city officers are appointed, *viz.*, the recorder, four common pleaders, the comptroller of the chamber, the two secondaries, the remembrancer, the city solicitor, the sword-bearer, the common hunt, the water bailiff, four attorneys of the Lord Mayor's Court, the clerk of the chamber, three sergeant carvers, three sergeants of the chamber, the sergeant of the chanel, the two marshals, the hall-keeper, the yeomen of the chamber, four yeomen of the waterside, the yeoman of the chanel, the under water-bailiff, two meal weighers, two fruit-meters, the foreign taker, the clerk of the City works, six young men, two clerks of the papers, eight attorneys of the Sheriff's Court, eight clerks fitters, two prothonotaries, the clerk of the Bridge House, the clerk of the Court of Requests, the beadle of the Court of Requests, thirty-six sergeants at mace, thirty-six yeomen, the gauger, the sealers and searchers of leather, the keeper of the Greenyard, two keepers of the two compters, the keeper of Newgate, the keeper of Ludgate, the measurer, the steward of Southwark (but the bailiff of Southwark is appointed by the Common Council) the bailiff of the hundred of Ossulston, the City artificers, and rent-gatherer, who hath been put in by Mr. Chamberlain.

In this court all leases and instruments that pass under the City Seal are executed; the assize of bread is settled by them; all differences relating to water-courses, lights, and party-walls, are determined, and officers are suspended or punished; and the aldermen, or a majority of them, have a negative in whatever is propounded in the Common Council.

2. The Court of Hustings is esteemed the most ancient tribunal in the City, and was established for the preservation of the laws, franchises, and customs of it. It is held at Guildhall before the Lord Mayor and Sheriffs, and in civil causes the Recorder sits as judge. Here deeds are enrolled, recoveries passed, writs of right, waste, partition, dower, and replevins determined.

3. The Lord Mayor's Court, a court of record, held in the chamber of Guildhall every Tuesday, where the Recorder also sits as judge, and the Lord Mayor and Aldermen may sit with him if they see fit. Actions of debt, trespass, arising within the City and liberties, of any value, may be tried in this court, and an action may be removed hither from the Sheriff's Court before the jury is sworn.

The juries for trying causes in this and the Sheriff's Courts, are returned by the several wards at their wardmote inquests at Christmas, when each ward appoints the persons to serve on juries for every month in the year ensuing.

44

This court is also a court of equity, and gives relief where judgment is obtained in the Sheriff's Court for more than the just debt.

4. The Sheriff's Courts are also courts of record, where may be tried actions of debt, trespass, covenant, &c. They are held on Wednesdays and Fridays for actions entered in Wood Street Compter, and every Thursday and Saturday for actions entered in the Poultry Compter. Here the testimony of an absent witness in writing is allowed to be good evidence.

5. The Chamberlain's Court or office is held at the chamber in Guildhall. He receives and pays the City cash and orphans' money, and keeps the securities taken by the Court of Aldermen for the same, and annually accounts to the auditors appointed for that purpose. He attends every morning at Guildhall, to enroll or turn over apprentices, or to make them free; and hears and determines differences between masters and their apprentices.

6. The Court of City Orphans is held by the Lord Mayor and Aldermen as often as occasion requires; the Common Sergeant being entrusted by them to take all inventories and accounts of freeman's estates, and the youngest attorney in the Mayor's Court is clerk of the orphans, and appointed to take security for their portions; for when any freeman dies, leaving children under the age of twenty-one years, the clerks of the respective parishes give in their names to the common crier, who thereupon summons the widow or executor to appear before the Court of Aldermen, to bring in an inventory, and give security for the testator's estate, for which they commonly allow two months' time, and in case of non-appearance, or refusal of security, the Lord Mayor may commit the executor to Newgate.

7. The Court of Conscience was established for recovering small debts under forty shillings at an easy expense, the creditor's oath of the debt being sufficient without further testimony to ascertain the debt. This court sits at the hustings in Guildhall every Wednesday and Saturday, where the Common Council of each ward are judges in their turns. They proceed first by summons, which costs but sixpence, and if the defendant appears there is no further charge; the debt is ordered to be paid at such times and in such proportion as the court in their consciences think the debtor able to discharge it; but if the defendant neglect to appear, or obey the order of the court, an attachment or execution follows with as much expedition and as small an expense as can be supposed. All persons within the freedom of the City, whether freemen or not, may prosecute and be prosecuted in this court, and freemen may be summoned who live out of the liberty.

8. The courts of wardmote are held by the aldermen of each ward, for choosing ward-officers, and settling the affairs of the ward, the Lord Mayor annually issuing his precept to the aldermen to hold his wardmote on St. Thomas's Day for the election of common councilmen and other officers; they also present such offences and nuisances at certain times to the Lord Mayor and common councilmen as require redress.

9. Small offences are punished by the justices in or out of sessions, by whom the offender is sentenced to be whipped, imprisoned, or kept to hard labour; but for the trial of capital offences, a commission of Oyer and Terminer and jail delivery issues eight times every year, *i.e.*, before and after every term, directed to the Lord Mayor, Recorder, some of the twelve judges, and others whom the Crown is pleased to assign. These commissioners sit at Justice Hall in the Old Bailey, and bills of indictment having been found by the grand juries of London or Middlesex, containing the prisoner's accusation, a petty jury, consisting of twelve substantial citizens is empanelled for the trial of each of them; for, as to the grand jury, they only consider whether there is such a probability of the prisoner's guilt as to put him upon making his defence, and this is determined by a majority of the grand jury: but the petty jury, who pass upon the prisoner's life and death, must all agree in their verdict, or he cannot be convicted. But though the petty jury judge of the fact, *i.e.*, what the crime is, or whether it was committed by the prisoner or not, the commissioners or judges declare what are the punishments appropriated to the several species of crimes, and pronounce judgment accordingly on the offender. In high treason they sentence the criminal to be drawn upon a hurdle to the place of execution, there to be hanged and quartered. In murder, robbery, and other felonies, which are excluded the benefit of the clergy, the criminal is sentenced to be hanged till he is dead. And for crimes within the benefit of the clergy, the offender is burnt in the hand or transported, at the discretion of the court. And for petty larceny, *i.e.*, where the offender is found guilty of theft under the value of twelve pence, he is sentenced to be whipped. But a report being made to His Majesty by the Recorder, of the circumstances with which the several capital offences were attended, and what may be urged either in aggravation or mitigation of them, the respective criminals are either pardoned or executed according to His Majesty's pleasure. But I should have remembered, that the sentence against a woman, either for high or petty treason, is to be burnt alive. I shall now give some account of the election of the Lord Mayor, Sheriffs, &c., who are chosen by a majority of the liverymen.

The Lord Mayor is elected on Michaelmas Day (from among the aldermen, by the liverymen of the City, who return two aldermen that have served sheriffs to the Court of Aldermen for their acceptance, who generally declare the first upon the liverymen's roll to be Lord-Mayor) sworn at Guildhall on Simon and Jude, and before the barons of the Exchequer at Westminster the day following.

The Lord Mayor appears abroad in very great state at all times, being clothed in scarlet robes, or purple richly furred, according to the season of the year, with a hood of black velvet, and a golden chain or collar of S.S. about his neck, and a rich jewel pendant thereon, his officers walking before and on both sides, his train held up, and the City sword and mace borne before him. He keeps open house during his mayoralty, and the sword-bearer is allowed 1,000 pounds for his table. The Lord Mayor usually goes to St. Paul's, attended by the aldermen in their gowns, and his officers, every Sunday morning; but especially the first Sunday in term-time, where he meets the twelve judges and invites them to dinner after divine service is ended.

The sheriffs are chosen into their office on Midsummer day annually by the liverymen also; to which end the Lord Mayor, aldermen, and sheriffs meet in the council-chamber at Guildhall, about eight in the morning, and coming down afterwards into the Court of Hustings, the recorder declares to the livery men assembled in the hall that this is the day prescribed for the election of these magistrates for the year ensuing: then the Court of Aldermen go up to the Lord Mayor's Court till the sheriffs are chosen; the old sheriffs, the chamberlain, common serjeant, town clerk, and other City officers remaining in the Court of Hustings, to attend the election. After the sheriffs are chosen, the commons proceed to elect a chamberlain, bridge-masters, auditors of the city and bridge-house accounts, and the surveyors of beer and ale, according to custom. The old sheriffs are judges of these elections, and declare by the common serjeant who are duly chosen. The sheriffs thus elected take the usual oaths in this court on Michaelmas eve, and the day after Michaelmas day are presented to the Barons of the Exchequer, where they take the oath of office, the oaths of allegiance, &c. The chamberlains and bridge-masters are sworn in the court of aldermen.

Where a Lord Mayor elect refuses to serve, he is liable to be fined; and if a person chosen sheriff refuses to serve, he is fined 413 pounds 6s. 8d., unless he makes oath he is not worth 10,000 pounds.

When the alderman of any ward dies, another is within a few days elected in his room, at a wardmote held for that purpose, at which the Lord Mayor usually presides. Every alderman has his deputy, who supplies his place in his absence. These deputies are always taken from among the Common Council. The aldermen above the chair, and the three eldest aldermen beneath it, are justices of peace in the City by the charter.

The Lord-Mayor's jurisdiction in some cases extends a great way beyond the City, upon the river Thames eastward as far as the conflux of the two rivers Thames and Medway, and up the river Lea as far as Temple Mills, being about three miles; and westward as far as Colney Ditch above Staine Bridge: he names a deputy called the water-bailiff, whose business is to prevent any encroachments, nuisances, and frauds used by fishermen or others, destructive to the fishery, or hurtful to the navigation of the said waters; and yearly keeps courts for the conservation of the river in the counties it borders upon within the said limits.

The sheriffs also are sheriffs of the county of Middlesex as well as of London. And here I shall take an opportunity to observe, that the number of aldermen are twenty-six; the number of Common-Council men two hundred and thirty-four; the number of companies eighty-four; and the number of citizens on the livery, who have a voice in their elections, are computed to be between seven and eight thousand. The twelve principal companies are:- 1. The Mercers; 2. Grocers; 3. Drapers; 4. Fishmongers; 5. Goldsmiths; 6. Skinners; 7. Merchant-Tailors; 8. Haberdashers; 9. Salters; 10. Ironmongers; 11. Vintners; 12. Clothworkers. The others:- are 13. The Dyers; 14. Brewers; 15. Leather-Sellers; 16. Pewterers; 17. Barber-Surgeons; 18. Cutlers; 19. Bakers; 20. Wax-Chandlers; 21. Tallow-Chandlers; 22. Armourers; 23. Girdlers;

24. Butchers; 25. Saddlers; 26. Carpenters; 27. Cord-wainers; 28. Painter-stainers; 29. Curriers; 30. Masons; 31. Plumbers; 32. Innholders; 33. Founders; 34. Poulterers; 35. Cooks; 36. Coopers; 37. Tilers and Bricklayers; 38. Bowyers; 39. Fletchers; 40. Blacksmiths; 41. Joiners; 42. Weavers; 43. Woolmen; 44. Scriveners; 45. Fruiterers; 46. Plasterers; 47. Stationers; 48. Embroiderers; 49. Upholders; 50. Musicians; 51. Turners; 52. *Basket-makers; 53. Glaziers; 54.* Horners; 55. Farriers; 56. *Paviours; 57. Lorimers; 58. Apothecaries; 59. Shipwrights; 60.* Spectacle-makers; 61. *Clock-makers; 62.* Glovers; 63. *Comb-makers; 64.* Felt-makers; 65. Frame-work Knitters; 66. *Silk throwers; 67. Carmen; 68.* Pin-makers; 69. Needle-makers; 70. Gardeners; 71. Soap-makers; 72. Tin-plate Workers; 73. Wheelwrights; 74. Distillers; 75. Hatband-makers; 76. Patten-makers; 77. Glasssellers; 78. Tobacco-pipe makers; 79. Coach and Coach-harness makers; 80. Gun-makers; 81. Gold and Silver Wire-Drawers; 82. Long Bow-string makers; 83. Card-makers; 84. Fan-makers.

The companies marked with an * before them have no liverymen, and all the freemen of the rest are not upon the livery, that is, entitled to wear the gowns belonging to the respective companies, and vote in elections, but a select number of freemen only. Every company is a distinct corporation, being incorporated by grants from the crown, or acts of parliament, and having certain rules, liberties, and privileges, for the better support and government of their several trades and mysteries: many of them are endowed with lands to a great value, and have their masters, wardens, assistants, clerks, and other officers, to direct and regulate their affairs, and to restrain and punish abuses incident to their several trades; and when any disputes arise concerning the due execution of these charters, the Lord Mayor has a supreme power to determine the case and to punish the offenders.

The military government of the City of London is lodged in the lieutenancy, consisting of the Lord Mayor, aldermen, and other principal citizens, who receive their authority from his majesty's commission, which he revokes and alters as often as he sees fit. These have under their command six regiments of foot, *viz.*:- 1, The White; 2, the Orange; 3, the Yellow; 4, the Blue; 5, the Green; and 6, the Red Regiment—in every one of which are eight companies, consisting of one hundred and fifty men each; in all, seven thousand two hundred men: besides which there is a kind of independent company, called the artillery company, consisting of seven or eight hundred volunteers, whose skill in military discipline is much admired by their fellow-citizens. These exercise frequently in the artillery ground, engage in mock fights and sieges, and storm the dunghills with great address.

The Tower Hamlets, it has been observed already, are commanded by the lieutenant of the Tower, and consist of two regiments of foot, eight hundred each: so that the whole militia of London, exclusive of Westminster and Southwark, amount to near ten thousand men.

London, like other cities of the kingdom, is, or ought to be, governed by its bishop in spirituals, though his authority is very little regarded at present. The justices of peace at their sessions may empower any man to preach and administer the sacraments, let his occupation or qualifications be never so mean; nor do they ever refuse it to a person who is able to raise the small sum of — pence being less a great deal than is paid for licensing a common alehouse. A clergyman indeed cannot be entitled to a benefice without being, in some measure, subject to his diocesan; but he may throw off his gown, and assemble a congregation that shall be much more beneficial to him, and propagate what doctrines he sees fit (as is evident in the case of orator Henley): but to proceed.

The diocese of London is in the province of Canterbury, and comprehends the counties of Middlesex and Essex, and part of Hertfordshire; the British plantations in America are also subject to this bishop. To the cathedral of St. Paul belongs a dean, three residentiaries, a treasurer, chancellor, precentor, and thirty prebendaries. The Bishop of London takes place next to the Archbishops of Canterbury and York, but his revenues are not equal to those of Durham or Winchester. The deanery of St. Paul's is said to be worth a thousand pounds per annum, and each of the residentiaries about three hundred pounds per annum.

The parishes within the walls of London are ninety-seven; but several of them having been united since the Fire, there are at present but sixty-two parish churches, and consequently the same number of parish priests: the revenues of these gentlemen are seldom less than 100 pounds per annum, and none more than 200 pounds per annum. They appear to be most of them about 150 pounds per annum, besides their several parsonage houses and surplice fees; and most of them have lectureships in town, or livings in the country, or some other spiritual preferment of equal value.

The city of Westminster, the western part of the town, comes next under consideration which received its name from the abbey or minster situated to the westward of London. This city, if we comprehend the district or liberties belonging to it, lies along the banks of the Thames in the form of a bow or crescent, extending from Temple Bar in the east to Millbank in the south-west; the inside of this bow being about a mile and a half in length, and the outside two miles and a half at least; the breadth, one place with another, from the Thames to the fields on the north-west side of the town, about a mile; and I am apt to think a square of two miles in length and one in breadth would contain all the buildings within the liberty of Westminster. That part of the town which is properly called the city of Westminster contains no more than St. Margaret's and St. John's parishes, which form a triangle, one side whereof extends from Whitehall to Peterborough House on Millbank; another side reaches from Peterborough House to Stafford House, or Tart Hall, at the west end of the park; and the third side extends from Stafford house to Whitehall; the circumference of the whole being about two miles. This spot of ground, it is said, was anciently an island, a branch of the Thames running through the park from west to east, and falling into the main river again about Whitehall, which island was originally called Thorney Island, from the woods and bushes that covered it; the abbey or minster also was at first called Thorney Abbey or minster, from the island on which it stood.

St. James's Park is something more than a mile in circumference, and the form pretty near oval; about the middle of it runs a canal 2,800 feet in length and 100 in breadth, and near it are several other waters, which form an island that has good cover for the breeding and harbouring wild ducks and other water-fowl; on the island also is a pretty house and garden, scarce visible to the company in the park. On the north side are several fine walks of elms and limes half a mile in length, of which the Mall is one. The palace of St. James's, Marlborough House, and the fine buildings in the street called Pall Mall, adorn this side of the park. At the east end is a view of the Admiralty, a magnificent edifice, lately built with brick and stone; the Horse Guards, the Banqueting House, the most elegant fabric in the kingdom, with the Treasury and the fine buildings about the Cockpit; and between these and the end of the grand canal is a spacious parade, where the horse and foot guards rendezvous every morning before they mount their respective guards.

On the south side of the park run shady walks of trees from east to west, parallel almost to the canal, and walks on the north; adjoining to which are the sumptuous houses in Queen Street, Queen Square, &c., inhabited by people of quality: and the west end of the park is adorned with the Duke of Buckingham's beautiful seat. But what renders St. James's Park one of the most delightful scenes in Nature is the variety of living objects which is met with here; for besides the deer and wild fowl, common to other parks, besides the water, fine walks, and the elegant buildings that surround it, hither the politest part of the British nation of both sexes frequently resort in the spring to take the benefit of the evening air, and enjoy the most agreeable conversation imaginable; and those who have a taste for martial music, and the shining equipage of the soldiery, will find their eyes and ears agreeably entertained by the horse and foot guards every morning.

The Sanctuary, or the abbey-yard, is a large open square, between King Street and the Gate-house, north-west of the abbey, and was called the Sanctuary, because any person who came within these limits was entitled to the privilege of sanctuary—that is, he was not liable to be apprehended by any officers of justice.

This privilege, it is said, was first granted to the abbey by Sebert, king of the East Saxons, increased by King Edgar, and confirmed by Edward the Confessor, by the following charter:-

"Edward, by the grace of God, king of Englishmen; I make it to be known to all generations of the world after me, that, by special commandment of our holy father Pope Leo, I have renewed and honoured the holy church of the blessed apostle St. Peter of Westminster; and I order and establish for ever, that what person, of what condition or estate soever he be, from whencesoever he come, or for what offence or cause it be, either for his refuge in the said holy place, he is assured of his life, liberty, and limbs: and over this, I forbid, under pain of everlasting damnation, that no minister of mine, or any of my successors, intermeddle with any of the goods, lands, and possessions of the said persons taking the said sanctuary: for I have taken their goods and livelode into my special protection. And therefore I grant to every, each of them, in as much as my terrestrial power may suffice, all manner of freedom of joyous liberty. And whosoever presumes, or doth contrary to this my grant, I will he lose his name, worship, dignity, and power; and that with the great traitor Judas that betrayed our Saviour, he be in the everlasting fire of hell. And I will and ordain, that this my grant endure as long as there remaineth in England either love or dread of Christian name."

This privilege of sanctuary, as far as it related to traitors, murderers, and felons, was in a great measure abolished by a statute of the 32nd Henry VIII.: and in the beginning of the reign of Queen Elizabeth, every debtor who fled to sanctuary, to shelter himself from his creditors, was obliged to take an oath of the following tenor, *viz.*:- That he did not claim the privilege of sanctuary to defraud any one of his goods, debts, or money, but only for the security of his person until he should be able to pay his creditors.

That he would give in a true particular of his debts and credits.

That he would endeavour to pay his debts as soon as possible.

That he would be present at the abbey at morning and evening prayer.

That he would demean himself honestly and quietly, avoid suspected houses, unlawful games, banqueting, and riotous company.

That he would wear no weapon, or be out of his lodging before sunrise or after sunset, nor depart out of the precinct of the sanctuary without the leave of the dean, or archdeacon in his absence.

That he would be obedient to the dean and the officers of the house.

And lastly, that if he should break his oath in any particular, he should not claim the privilege of sanctuary.

And if any creditor could make it appear that he had any money, goods, or chattels that were not contained in the particular given in to the dean and the church, the sanctuary man was to be imprisoned till he came to an agreement with his creditors.

The Abbey-Church of St. Peter at Westminster appears to be very ancient, though far from being so ancient as is vulgarly reported.

Some relate, without any authority to support the conjecture, that it was founded in the days of the Apostles by St. Peter himself; others that it was erected by King Lucius about the year 170. And by some it is said to have been built by King Sebert, the first Christian king of the East-Saxons (Essex and Middlesex), anno 611. But I take it for granted the church was not built before the convent or abbey it belonged to. People did not use to build churches at a distance from town, unless for the service of convents or religious houses. But neither in the times of the Apostles, nor in the supposed reign of King Lucius, in the second century, was there any such thing as a convent in England, or perhaps in any part of Christendom. During the dominion of the Saxons in this island, monasteries indeed were erected here, and in many other kingdoms, in great abundance; and as the monks generally chose thick woods or other solitary places for their residence, where could they meet with a spot of ground fitter for their purpose than this woody island called Thorney, then destitute of inhabitants? But I am inclined to think that neither this or any other monastery was erected in South Britain till the seventh century, after Austin the monk came into England. As to the tradition of its having been built upon the ruins of the temple of Apollo, destroyed by an earthquake, I do not doubt but the monks were very ready to propagate a fable of this kind, who formed so many others to show the triumphs of Christianity over paganism, and to induce their proselytes to believe that heaven miraculously interposed in their favour by earthquakes, storms, and other prodigies. But to proceed. When the convent was erected, I make no doubt that there was a church or chapel built as usual for the service of the monks; but it is evident from history that the dimensions of the first or second church that stood here were not comparable to those of the present church.

We may rely upon it that about the year 850 there was a church and convent in the island of Thorney, because about that time, London being in the possession of the Danes, the convent was destroyed by them (not in the year 659, as some writers have affirmed, because the Danes did not invade England till nearly 200 years afterwards). The abbey lay in ruins about a hundred years, when King Edgar, at the instance of Dunstan, Abbot of Glastonbury (and afterwards Archbishop of Canterbury), rebuilt this and several other monasteries, about the year 960. Edward the Confessor, a devout prince, enlarged this church and monastery, in which he placed the Benedictine monks, ordered the regalia to be kept by the fathers of the convent, and succeeding kings to be crowned here, as William the Conqueror and several other English monarchs afterwards were, most of them enriching this abbey with large revenues; but King Henry III. ordered the church built by Edward the Confessor to be pulled down, and erected the present magnificent fabric in the room of it, of which he laid the first stone about the year 1245.

That admired piece of architecture at the east end, dedicated to the Virgin Mary, was built by Henry VII., anno 1502, and from the founder is usually called Henry the VII.'s Chapel. Here most of the English monarchs since that time have been interred.

The dimensions of the abbey-church, according to the new survey, are as follows, viz.:- The length of the church, from the west end of it to the east end of St. Edward's Chapel, is 354 feet; the breadth of the west end, 66 feet; the breadth of the cross aisle, from north to south, 189 feet; the height of the middle roof, 92 feet; the distance from the west end of the church to the choir, 162 feet; and from the west end to the cross aisle, 220 feet; the distance from the east end of St. Edward's Chapel to the west end of Henry VII.'s Chapel, 36 feet; and the length of Henry VII.'s Chapel, 99 feet: so that the length of the whole building is 489 feet; the breadth of Henry VII.'s Chapel, 66 feet; and the height, 54 feet. The nave and cross aisles of the abbey-church are supported by fifty slender pillars, of Sussex marble, besides forty-five demi-pillars or pilasters. There are an upper and lower range of windows, being ninety-four in number, those at the four ends of the cross very spacious. All which, with the arches, roofs, doors, &c., are of the ancient Gothic order. Above the chapiters the pillars spread into several semi-cylindrical branches, forming and adorning the arches of the pillars, and those of the roofs of the aisles, which are three in number, running from east to west, and a cross aisle running from north to south. The choir is paved with black and white marble, in which are twenty-eight stalls on the north side, as many on the fourth, and eight at the west end; from the choir we ascend by several steps to a most magnificent marble altarpiece, which would be esteemed a beauty in an Italian church.

Beyond the altar is King Edward the Confessor's Chapel, surrounded with eleven or twelve other chapels replenished with monuments of the British nobility, for a particular whereof I refer the reader to the "Antiquities of St. Peter, or the Abbey-Church of Westminster," by J. Crull, M.D. Lond. 1711, 8vo, and the several supplements printed since; and shall only take notice of those of the kings and queens in the chapel of St. Edward the Confessor, which are as follows, viz., Edward I., King of England; Henry III.; Matilda, wife of Henry I.; Queen Eleanor, wife of Edward I.; St. Edward the Confessor, and Queen Editha, his wife; Henry V., and Queen Catherine of Valois, his wife; Edward III., and Queen Philippa, his wife; Richard II., and Queen Anne, his wife. And on the south side of the choir, King Sebert, and Queen Anne of Cheve, wife to Henry VIII. East of St. Edward's Chapel is that of Henry VII., dedicated to the blessed Virgin Mary, to which we ascend by twelve stone steps. At the west end whereof are three brazen doors finely wrought, which give an entrance into it. The stalls on the north and south sides are exquisitely carved. The roof is supported by twelve pillars and arches of the Gothic order, abounding with enrichments of carved figures, fruit, &c. At the east end is a spacious window with stained glass, besides which there are thirteen other windows above, and as many below on the north and south sides. Under each of the thirteen uppermost windows are five figures placed in niches, representing kings, queens, bishops, &c., and under them the figures of as many angels supporting imperial crowns. The roof, which is all stone, is divided into sixteen circles, curiously wrought, and is the admiration of all that see it.

The outside of this chapel was adorned with fourteen towers, three figures being placed in niches on each of them, which were formerly much admired; but the stone decaying and mouldering away, they make but an odd appearance at present.

In this chapel have been interred most of the English kings since Richard III., whose tombs are no small ornament to it, particularly that of Henry VII., the founder, which stands in the middle of the area towards the east end.

The tomb is composed of a curious pedestal whose sides are adorned with various figures, as the north with those of six men, the east with those of two cupids supporting the king's arms and an imperial crown; on the south side, also, six figures, circumscribed—as those on the north side—with circles of curious workmanship, the most easterly of which contains the figure of an angel treading on a dragon. Here is also a woman and a child, seeming to allude to Rev. xii.; and on the west end the figure of a rose and an imperial crown, supported with those of a dragon and a greyhound: on the tomb are the figures of the king and queen, lying at full length, with four angels, one at each angle of the tomb, all very finely done in brass.

The screen or fence is also of solid brass, very strong and spacious, being in length 19 feet, in breadth 11, and the altitude 11, adorned with forty-two pillars and their arches; also, twenty smaller hollow columns and their arches in the front of the former, and joined at the cornice, on which cornice is a kind of acroteria, enriched with roses and portcullises interchanged in the upper part, and with the small figures of dragons and greyhounds (the supporters aforesaid) in the lower part; and at each of the four angles is a strong pillar made open, or hollow, composed in imitation of diaper and Gothic archwork; the four sides have been adorned with thirty-two figures of men, about a cubit high, placed in niches, of which there are only seven left, the rest being stolen away (one Raymond, about the 11th of Queen Elizabeth, having been twice indicted for the same); and about the middle of the upper part of each of the four sides is a spacious branch adorned with the figure of a rose, where might on occasion be placed lamps. This admirable piece of art is open at top, and has two portals, one on the north, the other on the south side, all of fine brass.

This Royal founder's epitaph:

Septimus Henricus tumulo requiescit in isto,
Qui regum splendor, lumen et orbis erat.
Rex vigil et sapiens, comes virtutis, amatur,
Egregius forma, strenuus atque potens.
Qui peperit pacem regno, qui bella peregit
Plurima, qui victor semper ab hoste redit,
Qui natas binis conjunxit regibus ambas,
Regibus et cunctis faedere junctus erat.

Qui sacrum hoc struxit templum, statuitque; sepulchrum
Pro se, proque sua conjuge, proque domo.
Lustra decem atque; annos tres plus compleverit annos,

Nam tribus octenis regia sceptra tulit;
Quindecies Domini centenus fluxerat annus,
Currebat nonus, cum venit atra dies;
Septima ter mensis lux tunc fulgebat Aprilis,
Cum clausit summum tanta corona diem.
Nulla dedere prius tantum sibi saecula regem
Anglia, vix similem posteriora dabunt.

Septimus hic situs est Henricus gloria regum
Cunctorum, ipsius qui tempestate fuerunt;

54

Ingenio atque; opibus gestarum et nomine rerum,
Accessere quibus naturae dona benignae:
Frontis honos facies augusta heroica forma,
Junctaque ei suavis conjux per pulchra pudica,
Et faecunda fuit; felices prole parentes,
Henricum quibus octavum terra Anglia debet.

Under the figure of the king.

Hic jacet Henricus ejus nominis septimus, Anglicae quondam rex, Edmundi Richmondiae comitis filius, qui die 22 Aug. Rex creatus, statim post apud Westmonasterium die 30 Octob. coronatur 1485. Moritur deinde 21 die Aprilis anno aetat. 53, regnavit annos 23, menses 8, minus uno die.

Under the queen's figure.

Hic jacet regina Elizabetha, Edvardi quarti quondam regis filia, Edvardi quinti regis quondam nominatur soror: Henrici septimi olim regis conjux, atque; Henrici octavi regis mater inclyta; obiit autem suum diem in turri Londoniarum die secund. Feb. anno Domini 1502, 37 annorum aetate functa.

The modern tombs in the abbey, best worth the viewing, are those of the duke of Newcastle, on the left hand as we enter the north door, of Sir Isaac Newton, at the west end of the choir, of Sir Godfrey Kneller, and Mr. Secretary Craggs at the west end of the abbey, of Mr. Prior among the poets at the door which faces the Old Palace Yard, of the Duke of Buckingham in Henry VII.th's chapel, and that of Doctor Chamberlain on the North side of the choir: most of these are admirable pieces of sculpture, and show that the statuary's art is not entirely lost in this country; though it must be confessed the English fall short of the Italians in this science.

Westminster Hall is one of the largest rooms in Europe, being two hundred and twenty-eight feet in length, fifty-six feet broad, and ninety feet high. The walls are of stone, the windows of the Gothic form, the floor stone, and the roof of timber covered with lead; and having not one pillar in it, is supported by buttresses. It is usually observed that there are no cobwebs ever seen in this hall, and the reason given for this is, that the timber of which the roof is composed is Irish oak, in which spiders will not harbour; but I am inclined to believe that this is a fact not to be depended on, for I find the timber for rebuilding and repairing the Palace of Westminster in the reign of Richard III. was brought from the forests in Essex; and as there is no colour from history to surmise that the timber of this hall was Irish oak, so is there no imaginable reason why timber should be fetched from another kingdom for the repair of the hall, when the counties of Middlesex and Essex were great part of them forest, and afforded timber enough to have built twenty such places; and we find that the timber of the Essex forests was in fact applied to the repairs of this palace; for it cannot be pretended that the present roof is the same that was erected by William Rufus when it was first built, it appearing that Richard II., about the year 1397, caused the old roof to be taken down and a new one made (as has been observed already) and this is probably the same we now see. Here are hung up as trophies, 138 colours, and 34 standards, taken from the French and Bavarians at Hochstadt, anno 1704.

The House of Lords, or chamber where the peers assemble in Parliament, is situated between the Old Palace Yard and the Thames. It is a spacious room, of an oblong form, at the south end whereof is the King's throne, to which he ascends by several steps: on the right hand of the throne is a seat for the Prince of Wales, and on the left another for the princes of the blood, and behind the throne the seats of the peers under age.

On the east side of the house, to the right of the throne, sit the archbishops and bishops; on the opposite side of the house sit the dukes, marquises, earls, and viscounts; and on forms crossing the area, the barons under the degree of viscounts.

Before the throne are three wool-sacks, or broad seats stuffed with wool, to put the Legislature in mind, it is said, that the right management of this trade is of the last importance to the kingdom. On the first of these wool-sacks, next to the throne, sits the Lord Chancellor, or Keeper, who is Speaker of the House of Peers; and on the other two, the Lord Chief Justices and the rest of the judges, with the Master of the Rolls, and the other Masters in Chancery: about the middle of the house, on the east side, is a chimney, where a fire is usually kept in the winter; and towards the north, or lower end of the house, is a bar that runs across it, to which the commons advance when they bring up bills or impeachments, or when the King sends for them, and without this bar the council and witnesses stand at trials before the peers. The house is at present hung with tapestry, containing the history of the defeat of the Spanish Armada, in the reign of Queen Elizabeth, anno 1588.

The house or chamber where the commons assemble is to the northward of the House of Lords, and stands east and west, as the other does north and south. The room is pretty near square, and towards the upper end is the Speaker's armed chair, to which he ascends by a step or two; before it is a table where the clerks sit, on which the mace lies when the Speaker is in the chair, and at other times the mace is laid under the table. On the north and south sides, and at the west end, are seats gradually ascending as in a theatre, and between the seats at the west end is the entrance by a pair of folding-doors. There are galleries also on the north, south, and west, where strangers are frequently admitted to hear the debates.

This room was anciently a chapel, founded by King Stephen about the year 1141, and dedicated to the Blessed Virgin; however, it obtained the name of St. Stephen's Chapel. It was rebuilt by King Edward III., anno 1347, who placed in it a dean, twelve secular canons, thirteen vicars, four clerks, five choristers, a verger, and a keeper of the chapel, and built them a convent, which extended along the Thames, endowing it with large revenues, which at the dissolution of monasteries in the reign of Edward VI. amounted to near eleven thousand pounds per annum. Almost ever since the dissolution, this chapel has been converted to the use we find it at present, *viz.*, for the session of the Lower House of Parliament, who, before that time, usually assembled in the chapter-house belonging to the Abbey, when the Parliament met at Westminster. The Painted Chamber lies between the House of Lords and the House of Commons, and here the committees of both houses usually meet at a conference; but neither this nor the other remaining apartments of this Palace of Westminster have anything in them that merit a particular description.

The open place usually called Charing Cross, from a fine cross which stood there before the grand rebellion, is of a triangular form, having the Pall Mall and the Haymarket on the north-west, the Strand on the east, and the street before Whitehall on the south. In the middle of this space is erected a brazen equestrian statue of King Charles I., looking towards the place where that prince was murdered by the rebels, who had erected a scaffold for that purpose before the gates of his own palace. This statue is erected on a stone pedestal seventeen feet high, enriched with his Majesty's arms, trophy-work, palm-branches, &c., enclosed with an iron palisade, and was erected by King Charles II. after his restoration. The brick buildings south-east of Charing Cross are mostly beautiful and uniform, and the King's stables in the Mews, which lie north of it, and are now magnificently rebuilding of hewn stone, will probably make Charing Cross as fine a place as any we have in town; especially as it stands upon an eminence overlooking Whitehall.

The Banqueting-house stands on the east side of the street adjoining to the great gate of Whitehall on the south. This edifice is built of hewn stone, and consists of one stately room, of an oblong form, upwards of forty feet in height, the length and breadth proportionable, having galleries round it on the inside, the ceiling beautifully painted by that celebrated history-painter, Sir Peter Paul Rubens: it is adorned on the outside with a lower and upper range of columns of the Ionic and Composite orders, their capitals enriched with fruit, foliage, &c., the intercolumns of the upper and lower range being handsome sashed windows. It is surrounded on the top with stone rails or banisters, and covered with lead.

St. James's Palace, where the Royal Family now resides in the winter season, stands pleasantly upon the north side of the Park, and has several noble rooms in it, but is an irregular building, by no means suitable to the grandeur of the British monarch its master. In the front next St. James's Street there appears little more than an old gate-house, by which we enter a little square court, with a piazza on the west side of it leading to the grand staircase; and there are two other courts beyond, which have not much the air of a prince's palace. This palace was a hospital, suppressed by Henry VIII., who built this edifice in the room of it.

But the house most admired for its situation is that of the Duke of Buckingham at the west end of the Park; in the front of which, towards the Mall and the grand canal, is a spacious court, the offices on each side having a communication with the house by two little bending piazzas and galleries that form the wings. This front is adorned with two ranges of pilasters of the Corinthian and Tuscan orders, and over them is an acroteria of figures, representing Mercury, Secrecy, Equity, and Liberty, and under them this inscription in large golden characters, *viz.*, *Sic* SITI LAETANTVR *Lares* (Thus situated, may the household gods rejoice).

Behind the house is a fine garden and terrace, from whence there is prospect adjacent on the house on that side, *viz.*, RVS *in* VRBE, intimating that it has the advantages both of city and country; above which are figures representing the four seasons: The hall is paved with marble, and adorned with pilasters, the intercolumns exquisite paintings in great variety; and on a pedestal, near the foot of the grand staircase, is a marble figure of Cain killing his brother Abel; the whole structure exceeding magnificent, rich, and beautiful, but especially in the finishing and furniture.

Grosvenor or Gravenor Square is bounded on the north by Oxford Road, on the east by Hanover Square, by Mayfair on the south, and by Hyde Park on the west; the area whereof contains about five acres of ground, in which is a large garden laid out into walks, and adorned with an equestrian statue of King George I. gilded with gold, and standing on a pedestal, in the centre of the garden, the whole surrounded with palisades placed upon a dwarf wall. The buildings generally are the most magnificent we meet with in this great town; though the fronts of the houses are not all alike, for some of them are entirely of stone, others of brick and stone, and others of rubbed brick, with only their quoins, fascias, windows, and door-cases of stone; some of them are adorned with stone columns of the several orders, while others have only plain fronts; but they are so far uniform as to be all sashed, and of pretty near an equal height. To the kitchens and offices, which have little paved yards with vaults before them, they descend by twelve or fifteen steps, and these yards are defended by a high palisade of iron. Every house has a garden behind it, and many of them coach-houses and stables adjoining; and others have stables near the square, in a place that has obtained the name of Grosvenor Mews. The finishing of the houses within is equal to the figure they make without; the staircases of some of them I saw were inlaid, and perfect cabinet-work, and the paintings on the roof and sides by the best hands. The apartments usually consist of a long range of fine rooms, equally commodious and beautiful; none of the houses are without two or three staircases for the convenience of the family. The grand staircase is generally in the hall or saloon at the entrance. In short, this square may well be looked upon as the beauty of the town, and those who have not seen it cannot have an adequate idea of the place.

The city of Westminster at this day consists of the parishes of St. Margaret and St. John the Evangelist, and the liberties of Westminster, *viz.*, St. Martin's-in-the-Fields; St. Mary le Savoy; St. Mary le Strand; St. Clement's Danes; St. Paul's, Covent Garden; St. James's, Westminster; St. George's, Hanover Square; and St. Anne's, Westminster; all under the government of the dean and chapter of Westminster, and their subordinate officers; or rather, of a high steward, and such other officers as are appointed by them; for since the Reformation, the dean and chapter seem to have delegated their civil power to such officers as they elect for life, who are not accountable to, or liable to be displaced by them, nor are they liable to forfeit their offices, but for such offences as a private man may lose his estate, namely, for high

58

treason, felony, &c., as happened in the case of their high steward, the Duke of Ormond, upon whose attainder the dean and chapter proceeded to a new election.

The next officer to the high steward is the deputy steward, appointed by the high steward, and confirmed by the dean and chapter, who is usually a gentleman learned in the law, being judge of their court for trial of civil actions between party and party, which is held usually on Wednesday every week. They have also a court-leet, held annually on St. Thomas's Day, for the choice of officers, and removal of nuisances. The deputy-steward supplies the place of sheriff of Westminster, except in the return of members of Parliament, which is done by the high bailiff, an officer nominated by the dean and chapter, and confirmed by the high steward. The high-bailiff also is entitled to all fines, forfeitures, waifs and strays in Westminster, which makes it a very profitable post.

The high constable, chosen by the burgesses at their court-leet, and approved by the steward or his deputy, is an officer of some consideration in this city also, to whom all the rest of the constables are subject.

The burgesses are sixteen in number, seven for the city and nine for the liberties of Westminster, appointed by the high steward or his deputy, every one of whom has his assistant, and has particular wards or districts: out of these burgesses are chosen two chief burgesses, one for the city, the other for the liberties. The dean, high steward, or his deputy, the bailiffs and burgesses, or a quorum of them, are empowered to make bye-laws, and take cognisance of small offences, within the city and liberties of Westminster. But I look upon it that the justices of peace for Westminster have in a great measure superseded the authority of the burgesses (except as to weights, measures, and nuisances), by virtue of whose warrants all petty offenders almost are apprehended and sent to Tothill Fields Bridewell; and for higher offences, the same justices commit criminals to Newgate, or the Gatehouse, who receive their trials before commissioners of oyer and terminer at the Old Bailey, as notorious criminals in the City of London do; and so far the two united cities may be said to be under the same government.

The precinct of St. Martin's-le-Grand, in London, is deemed a part of the city of Westminster, and the inhabitants vote in the elections of members of Parliament for Westminster.

The ecclesiastical government of the city of Westminster is in the dean, and chapter, whose commissary has the jurisdiction in all ecclesiastical causes, and the probate of wills; from whom there lies no appeal to the Archbishop of Canterbury or other spiritual judge, but to the King in Chancery alone, who upon such appeal issues a commission under the Great Seal of England, constituting a court of delegates to determine the cause finally.

I next proceed to survey the out-parishes in the Counties of Middlesex and Surrey which are comprehended within the bills of mortality, and esteemed part of this great town. And first, St. Giles's in the Fields contains these chief streets and places:

Great Lincoln's Inn Fields, part of Lincoln's Inn Garden, Turnstile, Whetstone Park, part of High Holborn, part of Duke Street, Old and New Wild Street, Princes Street, Queen Street, part of Drury Lane, Brownlow Street, Bolton Street, Castle Street, King Street, the Seven Dials, or seven streets comprehending Earl Street, Queen Street, White Lion Street, and St. Andrew's Street, Monmouth Street, the east side of Hog Lane, Stedwell Street, and Staig Street.

Great Lincoln's Inn Fields or Square contains about ten acres of ground, and is something longer than it is broad, the longest sides extending from east to west. The buildings on the west and south generally make a grand figure.

In the parish of St. Sepulchre, which is without the liberties of the City of London, we meet with Hicks's Hall and the Charter House.

Hicks's Hall is situated in the middle of St. John's Street, towards the south end, and is the sessions house for the justices of peace of the County of Middlesex, having been erected for this end, anno 1612, by Sir Baptist Hicks, a mercer in Cheapside, then a justice of the peace. The justices before holding their sessions at the Castle Inn, near Smithfield Bars.

To the eastward of Hicks's Hall stood the late dissolved monastery of the Charter House, founded by Sir Walter Manny, a native of the Low Countries, knighted by King Edward III. for services done to this crown, probably in the wars against France.

Sir Walter Manny at first erected only a chapel, and assigned it to be the burial-place of all strangers; but in the year 1371 Sir Walter founded a monastery of Carthusian monks here, transferring to these fathers thirteen acres and a rood of land with the said chapel: the revenues of which convent, on the dissolution of monasteries, 30 Henry VIII., amounted to 642 pounds 4d. 1ob. per annum.

Sir Thomas Audley soon after obtained a grant of this Carthusian monastery, together with Duke's Place, and gave the former in marriage with his daughter Margaret to Thomas, Duke of Norfolk, from whom it descended to the Earl of Suffolk, and was called Howard House, the surname of that noble family. By which name Thomas Sutton, Esq., purchased it of the Earl of Suffolk for 13,000 pounds, anno 1611, and converted it into a hospital by virtue of letters patent obtained from King James I., which were afterwards confirmed by Act of Parliament, 3 Charles I.

Pounds s. d. The manors, lands, tenements, and hereditaments which the founder settled upon this hospital amounted to, per annum 4493 19 10 The revenues purchased by his executors, &c., after his death, to per annum 897 13 9 Total of the charity per annum 5391 13 7

But the revenues now amount to upwards of 6,000 pounds per annum by the improvement of the rents. This charity was given for the maintenance of fourscore old men, who were to be either gentlemen by descent reduced to poverty, soldiers by sea or land, merchants who had suffered by piracy or shipwreck, or servants of the King's household, and were to be fifty years of age and upwards at their admission, except maimed soldiers, who are capable of being admitted at forty years of age. Nor are any to be admitted who are afflicted with leprosy, or any unclean or infectious disease, or who shall be possessed of the value of 200 pounds, or 14 pounds per annum for life, or who are married men. No poor brother to go beyond sea without the licence of six of the governors, nor to go into the country for above two months without the master's leave, and during such absence shall be allowed but two-thirds of his commons in money besides his salary; and if a brother go out and is arrested he shall have no allowance during his absence, but his place to be reserved till the governors' pleasure be known.

No brother to pass the gates of the hospital in his livery gown, or to lie out of the house, or solicit causes, or molest any of the King's subjects, under a certain pecuniary pain; and all other duties, such as frequenting chapel, decent clothing and behaviour, to be regulated by the governors.

This munificent benefactor also founded a grammar school in the Charter House, to consist of a master, usher, and forty scholars.

No scholars to be admitted at above fourteen or under ten years of age.

The scholars are habited in black gowns, and when any of them are fit for the university, and are elected, each of them receives 20 pounds per annum for eight years out of the revenues of the house. And such boys who are found more fit for trades are bound out, and a considerable sum of money given with them.

When any of the forty boys are disposed of, or any of the old men die, others are placed in their rooms by the governors in their turns.

The master is to be an unmarried man, aged about forty; one that hath no preferment in Church or State which may draw him from his residence and care of the hospital.

The preacher must be a Master of Arts, of seven years' standing in one of the universities of England, and one who has preached four years.

The governors meet in December, to take the year's accounts, view the state of the hospital, and to determine other affairs; and again in June or July, to dispose of the scholars to the university or trades, make elections, &c. And a committee of five at the least is appointed at the assembly in December yearly, to visit the school between Easter and Midsummer, &c.

The buildings of the Charter House take up a great deal of ground, and are commodious enough, but have no great share of beauty. This house has pretty much the air of a college or monastery, of which the principal rooms are the chapel and the hall; and the old men who are members of the society have their several cells, as the monks have in Portugal.

The chapel is built of brick and boulder, and is about sixty-three feet in length, thirty-eight in breadth, and twenty-four in height. Here Sir William Manny, founder of the Carthusian monastery, was buried; and here was interred Mr. Sutton, the founder of the hospital, whose monument is at the north-east angle of the chapel, being of black and white marble, adorned with four columns, with pedestals and entablature of the Corinthian order, between which lies his effigy at length in a fur gown, his face upwards and the palms of his hands joined over his breast; and on the tomb is the following inscription:-

"Sacred to the glory of God, in grateful memory of Thomas Sutton, Esq. Here lieth buried the body of Thomas Sutton, late of Castle Camps, in the County of Cambridge, Esq., at whose only cost and charges this Hospital was founded and endowed with large possessions, for the relief of poor men and children. He was a gentleman born at Knayth, in the County of Lincoln, of worthy and honest parentage. He lived to the age of seventy-nine years, and deceased the 12th day of December, 1611."

The Charter House gardens are exceeding pleasant, and of a very great extent, considering they stand so far within this great town.

I shall, in the next place, survey the free schools and charity schools.

Anciently I have read that there were three principal churches in London that had each of them a famous school belonging to it; and these three churches are supposed to be—(1) The Cathedral Church of St. Paul, because, at a general council holden at Rome, anno 1176, it was decreed, "That every cathedral church should have its schoolmaster, to teach poor scholars and others as had been accustomed, and that no man should take any reward for licence to teach." (2) The Abbey Church of St Peter at Westminster; for of the school here Ingulphus, Abbot of Croyland, in the reign of William the Conqueror, writes as follows: "I, Ingulphus, a humble servant of God, born of English parents, in the most beautiful city of London, for attaining to learning was first put to Westminster, and after to study at Oxford," &c. (3) The Abbey Church of St. Saviour, at Bermondsey, in Southwark; for this is supposed to be the most ancient and most considerable monastery about the city at that time, next to that of St. Peter at Westminster, though there is no doubt but the convents of St. John by Clerkenwell, St. Bartholomew in Smithfield, St. Mary Overy in Southwark, that of the Holy Trinity by Aldgate, and other monasteries about the city, had their respective schools, though not in such reputation as the three first. Of these none are now existing but St. Paul's and Westminster, though perhaps on different and later foundations. Yet other schools have been erected in this metropolis from time to time, amongst which I find that called Merchant Taylors' to be the most considerable.

St. Paul's School is situated on the east side of St. Paul's Churchyard, being a handsome fabric built with brick and stone, founded by John Collet, D.D. and Dean of St. Paul's, anno 1512, who appointed a high-master, sur-master, a chaplain or under-master, and 153 scholars, to be taught by them gratis, of any nation or country. He also left some exhibitions to such scholars as are sent to the universities and have continued at this school three years. The masters are elected by the wardens and assistants of the Mercers' Company, and the scholars are admitted by the master upon a warrant directed to him by the surveyor. The elections for the university are in March, before Lady Day, and they are allowed their exhibitions for seven years. To this school belongs a library, consisting chiefly of classic authors. The frontispiece is adorned with busts, entablature, pediments, festoons, shields, vases, and the Mercers' arms cut in stone, with this inscription over the door: INGREDERE UT PROFICIAS. Upon every window of the school was written, by the founder's direction: AUT DOCE, AUT DISCE, AUT DISCEDE—i.e., Either teach, learn, or begone.

The founder, in the ordinances to be observed in this school, says he founded it to the honour of the Child Jesus, and of His blessed mother Mary; and directs that the master be of a healthful constitution, honest, virtuous, and learned in Greek and Latin; that he be a married or single man, or a priest that hath no cure; that his wages should be a mark a week, and a livery gown of four nobles, with a house in town, and another at Stebonheath (Stepney); that there should be no play-days granted but to the King, or some bishop in person: that the scholars every Childermas Day should go to St. Paul's Church, and hear the child-bishop sermon, and afterwards at high mass each of them offer a penny to the child-bishop: and committed the care of the school to the Company of Mercers; the stipends to the masters, the officers' salaries, &c., belonging to the school, amounting at first to 118 pounds 14s. 7d. 1ob. per annum; but the rents and revenues of the school being of late years considerably advanced, the salaries of the masters have been more than doubled, and many exhibitions granted to those who go to the university, of 10 pounds and 6 pounds odd money per annum. The second master hath a handsome house near the school, as well as the first master.

The school at Mercers' Chapel, in Cheapside, hath the same patrons and governors as that of St. Paul's, *viz.*, the Mercers, who allow the master a salary of 40 pounds per annum, and a house, for teaching twenty-five scholars gratis.

Merchant Taylors' School is situated near Cannon Street, on St. Lawrence Poultney (or Pountney) Hill. This school, I am told, consists of six forms, in which are three hundred lads, one hundred of whom are taught gratis, another hundred pay two shillings and sixpence per quarter, and the third hundred five shillings a quarter; for instructing of whom there is a master and three ushers: and out of these scholars some are annually, on St. Barnabas' Day, the 11th of June, elected to St. John's College, in Oxford, where there are forty-six fellowships belonging to the school.

As to the charity schools: there are in all 131, some for boys, others for girls; where the children are taught, if boys, to read, write, and account; if girls, to read, sew, and knit; who are all clothed and fitted for service or trades gratis.

I proceed in the next place to show how well London is supplied with water, firing, bread-corn, flesh, fish, beer, wine, and other provisions.

And as to water, no city was ever better furnished with it, for every man has a pipe or fountain of good fresh water brought into his house, for less than twenty shillings a year, unless brewhouses, and some other great houses and places that require more water than an ordinary family consumes, and these pay in proportion to the quantity they spend; many houses have several pipes laid in, and may have one in every room, if they think fit, which is a much greater convenience than two or three fountains in a street, for which some towns in other countries are so much admired.

These pipes of water are chiefly supplied from the waterworks at London Bridge, Westminster, Chelsea, and the New River.

Besides the water brought from the Thames and the New River, there are a great many good springs, pumps, and conduits about the town, which afford excellent water for drinking. There are also mineral waters on the side of Islington and Pancras.

This capital also is well supplied with firing, particularly coals from Newcastle, and pit-coals from Scotland, and other parts; but wood is excessively dear, and used by nobody for firing, unless bakers, and some few persons of quality in their chambers and drawing-rooms.

As for bread-corn, it is for the most part brought to London after it is converted into flour, and both bread and flour are extremely reasonable: we here buy as much good white bread for three-halfpence or twopence, as will serve an Englishman a whole day, and flour in proportion. Good strong beer also may be had of the brewer, for about twopence a quart, and of the alehouses that retail it for threepence a quart. Bear Quay, below bridge, is a great market for malt, wheat, and horse-corn; and Queenhithe, above the bridge, for malt, wheat, flour, and other grain.

The butchers here compute that there are about one thousand oxen sold in Smithfield Market one week with another the year round; besides many thousand sheep, hogs, calves, pigs, and lambs, in this and other parts of the town; and a great variety of venison, game, and poultry. Fruit, roots, herbs, and other garden stuff are very cheap and good.

Fish also are plentiful, such as fresh cod, plaice, flounders, soles, whitings, smelts, sturgeon, oysters, lobsters, crabs, shrimps, mackerel, and herrings in the season; but it must be confessed that salmon, turbot, and some other sea-fish are dear, as well as fresh-water fish.

Wine is imported from foreign countries, and is dear. The port wine which is usually drunk, and is the cheapest, is two shillings a quart, retailed in taverns, and not much less than eighteen or twenty pounds the hogshead, when purchased at the best hand; and as to French wines, the duties are so high upon them that they are double the price of the other at least. White wine is about the same price as red port, and canary about a third dearer.

It is computed that there are in London some part of the year, when the nobility and gentry are in town, 15,000 or 16,000 large horses for draught, used in coaches, carts, or drays, besides some thousands of saddle-horses; and yet is the town so well supplied with hay, straw, and corn, that there is seldom any want of them. Hay generally is not more than forty shillings the load, and from twenty pence to two shillings the bushel is the usual price of oats.

The opportunity of passing from one part of the town to the other, by coach, chair, or boat, is a very great convenience, especially in the winter, or in very hot weather. A servant calls a coach or a chair in any of the principal streets, which attends at a minute's warning, and carries one to any part of the town, within a mile and a half distance, for a shilling, but to a chair is paid one-third more; the coaches also will wait for eighteenpence the first hour, and a shilling every succeeding hour all day long; or you may hire a coach and a pair of horses all day, in or out of town, for ten shillings per day; there are coaches also that go to every village almost about town, within four or five miles, in which a passenger pays but one shilling, and in some but sixpence, for his passage with other company.

The pleasantest way of moving from one end of the town to the other in summer time is by water, on that spacious gentle stream the Thames, on which you travel two miles for sixpence, if you have two watermen, and for threepence if you have but one; and to any village up or down the river you go with company for a trifle. But the greatest advantage reaped from this noble river is that it brings whatever this or other countries afford. Down the river from Oxfordshire, Berkshire, Bucks, &c., come corn and all manner of provision of English growth, as has been observed already; and up the river, everything that the coasts and the maritime counties of England, Scotland, or Ireland afford; this way also are received the treasures and merchandise of the East and West Indies, and indeed of the four quarters of the world.

Carts are hired as coaches, to remove goods and merchandise from one part of the town to the other, whose rates are also fixed, and are very reasonable; and for small burdens or parcels, and to send on messages, there are porters at every corner of the streets, those within the City of London and liberties thereof being licensed by authority, and wearing a badge or ticket; in whose hands goods of any value, and even bills of exchange or sums of money, may be safely trusted, they being obliged at their admission to give security. There is also a post that goes from one part of the town to the other several times a day; and once a day to the neighbouring villages, with letters and small parcels; for the carriage of which is given no more than a penny the letter or parcel. And I should have remembered that every coach, chair, and boat that plies for hire has its number upon it; and if the number be taken by any friend or servant, at the place you set out from, the proprietor of the vehicle will be obliged to make good any loss or damage that may happen to the person carried in it, through the default of the people that carry him, and to make him satisfaction for any abuse or ill-language he may receive from them.

The high streets from one end of the town to the other are kept clean by scavengers in the winter, and in summer the dust in some wide streets is laid by water-carts: they are so wide and spacious, that several lines of coaches and carts may pass by each other without interruption. Foot-passengers in the high streets go about their business with abundance of ease and pleasure; they walk upon a fine smooth pavement; defended by posts from the coaches and wheel-carriages; and though they are jostled sometimes in the throng, yet as this seldom happens out of design, few are offended at it; the variety of beautiful objects, animate and inanimate, he meets with in the streets and shops, inspires the passenger with joy, and makes him slight the trifling inconvenience of being crowded now and then. The lights also in the shops till eight or nine in the evening, especially in those of toymen and pastry-cooks, in the winter, make the night appear even brighter and more agreeable than the day itself.

From the lights I come very naturally to speak of the night-guards or watch. Each watch consists of a constable and a certain number of watchmen, who have a guard-room or watch-house in some certain place, from whence watchmen are despatched every hour, to patrol in the streets and places in each constable's district; to see if all be safe from fire and thieves; and as they pass they give the hour of the night, and with their staves strike at the door of every house.

If they meet with any persons they suspect of ill designs, quarrelsome people, or lewd women in the streets, they are empowered to carry them before the constable at his watch-house, who confines them till morning, when they are brought before a justice of the peace, who commits them to prison or releases them, according as the circumstances of the case are.

Mobs and tumults were formerly very terrible in this great city; not only private men have been insulted and abused, and their houses demolished, but even the Court and Parliament have been influenced or awed by them. But there is now seldom seen a multitude of people assembled, unless it be to attend some malefactor to his execution, or to pelt a villain in the pillory, the last of which being an outrage that the Government has ever seemed to wink at; and it is observed by some that the mob are pretty just upon these occasions; they seldom falling upon any but notorious rascals, such as are guilty of perjury, forgery, scandalous practices, or keeping of low houses, and these with rotten eggs, apples, and turnips, they frequently maul unmercifully, unless the offender has money enough to bribe the constables and officers to protect him.

The London inns, though they are as commodious for the most part as those we meet with in other places, yet few people choose to take up their quarters in them for any long time; for, if their business requires them to make any stay in London, they choose to leave their horses at the inn or some livery-stable, and take lodgings in a private house. At livery stables they lodge no travellers, only take care of their horses, which fare better here than usually at inns; and at these places it is that gentlemen hire saddle-horses for a journey. At the best of them are found very good horses and furniture: they will let out a good horse for 4s. a day, and an ordinary hackney for 2s. 6d., and for 5s. you may have a hunter for the city hounds have the liberty of hunting; in Enfield Chase and round the town, and go out constantly every week in the season, followed by a great many young gentlemen and tradesmen. They have an opportunity also of hunting with the King's hounds at Richmond and Windsor: and such exercises seem very necessary for people who are constantly in London, and eat and drink as plentifully as any people in the world. And now I am speaking of hired horses, I cannot avoid taking notice of the vast number of coach-horses that are kept to be let out to noblemen or gentlemen, to carry or bring them to and from the distant parts of the kingdom, or to supply the undertakers of funerals with horses for their coaches and hearses. There are some of these men that keep several hundreds of horses, with coaches, coachmen, and a complete equipage, that will be ready at a day's warning to attend a gentleman to any part of England. These people also are great jockeys. They go to all the fairs in the country and buy up horses, with which they furnish most of the nobility and gentry about town. And if a nobleman does not care to run any hazard, or have the trouble of keeping horses in town, they will agree to furnish him with a set all the year round.

The principal taverns are large handsome edifices, made as commodious for the entertaining a variety of company as can be contrived, with some spacious rooms for the accommodation of numerous assemblies. Here a stranger may be furnished with wines, and excellent food of all kinds, dressed after the best manner:- each company, and every particular man, if he pleases, has a room to himself, and a good fire if it be winter time, for which he pays nothing, and is not to be disturbed or turned out of his room by any other man of what quality soever, till he thinks fit to leave it. And as many people meet here upon business, at least an equal-number resort hither purely for pleasure, or to refresh themselves in an evening after a day's fatigue.

And though the taverns are very numerous, yet ale-houses are much more so, being visited by the inferior tradesmen, mechanics, journeymen, porters, coachmen, carmen, servants, and others whose pockets will not reach a glass of wine. Here they sit promiscuously in common dirty rooms, with large fires, and clouds of tobacco, where one that is not used to them can scarce breathe or see; but as they are a busy sort of people, they seldom stay long, returning to their several employments, and are succeeded by fresh sets of the same rank of men, at their leisure hours, all day long.

Of eating-houses and cook-shops there are not many, considering the largeness of the town, unless it be about the Inns of Court and Chancery, Smithfield, and the Royal Exchange, and some other places, to which the country-people and strangers resort when they come to town. Here is good butcher's meat of all kinds, and in the best of them fowls, pigs, geese, &c., the last of which are pretty dear; but one that can make a meal of butcher's meat, may have as much as he cares to eat for sixpence; he must be content indeed to sit in a public room, and use the same linen that forty people have done before him. Besides meat, he finds very good white bread, table-beer, &c.

Coffee-houses are almost as numerous as ale-houses, dispersed in every part of the town, where they sell tea, coffee, chocolate, drams, and in many of the great ones arrack and other punch, wine, &c. These consist chiefly of one large common room, with good fires in winter; and hither the middle sort of people chiefly resort, many to breakfast, read the news, and talk politics; after which they retire home: others, who are strangers in town, meet here about noon, and appoint some tavern to dine at; and a great many attend at the coffee-houses near the Exchange, the Inns of Court, and Westminster, about their business. In the afternoon about four, people resort to these places again, from whence they adjourn to the tavern, the play, &c.; and some, when they have taken a handsome dose, run to the coffee-house at midnight for a dish of coffee to set them right; while others conclude the day here with drams, or a bowl of punch.

There are but few cider-houses about London, though this be liquor of English growth, because it is generally thought too cold for the climate, and to elevate the spirits less than wine or strong beer.

The four grand distinctions of the people are these:- (1) The nobility and gentry; (2) the merchants and first-rate tradesmen; (3) the lawyers and physicians; and (4) inferior tradesmen, attorneys, clerks, apprentices, coachmen, carmen, chairmen, watermen, porters, and servants.

The first class may not only be divided into nobility and gentry, but into either such as have dependence on the Court, or such as have none. Those who have offices, places, or pensions from the Court, or any expectations from thence, constantly attend the levees of the prince and his ministers, which takes up the greatest part of the little morning they have. At noon most of the nobility, and such gentlemen as are members of the House of Commons, go down to Westminster, and when the Houses do not sit late, return home to dinner. Others that are not members of either House, and have no particular business to attend, are found in the chocolate-houses near the Court, or in the park, and many more do not stir from their houses till after dinner. As to the ladies, who seldom rise till about noon, the first part of their time is spent, after the duties of the closet, either at the tea-table or in dressing, unless they take a turn to Covent Garden or Ludgate Hill, and tumble over the mercers' rich silks, or view some India or China trifle, some prohibited manufacture, or foreign lace.

Thus, the business of the day being despatched before dinner, both by the ladies and gentlemen, the evening is devoted to pleasure; all the world get abroad in their gayest equipage between four and five in the evening, some bound to the play, others to the opera, the assembly, the masquerade, or music-meeting, to which they move in such crowds that their coaches can scarce pass the streets.

The merchants and tradesmen of the first-rate make no mean figure in London; they have many of them houses equal to those of the nobility, with great gates and courtyards before them, and seats in the country, whither they retire the latter end of the week, returning to the city again on Mondays or Tuesdays; they keep their coaches, saddle-horses, and footmen; their houses are richly and beautifully furnished; and though their equipage be not altogether so shining and their servants so numerous as those of the nobility, they generally abound in wealth and plenty, and are generally masters of a larger cash than they have occasion to make use of in the way of trade, whereby they are always provided against accidents, and are enabled to make an advantageous purchase when it offers. And in this they differ from the merchants of other countries, that they know when they have enough, for they retire to their estates, and enjoy the fruits of their labours in the decline of life, reserving only business enough to divert their leisure hours. They become gentlemen and magistrates in the counties where their estates lie, and as they are frequently the younger brothers of good families, it is not uncommon to see them purchase those estates that the eldest branches of their respective families have been obliged to part with.

Their character is that they are neither so much in haste as the French to grow rich, nor so niggardly as the Dutch to save; that their houses are richly furnished, and their tables well served. You are neither soothed nor soured by the merchants of London; they seldom ask too much, and foreigners buy of them as cheap as others. They are punctual in their payments, generous and charitable, very obliging, and not too ceremonious; easy of access, ready to communicate their knowledge of the respective countries they traffic with, and the condition of their trade.

As to their way of life, they usually rise some hours before the gentlemen at the other end of the town, and having paid their devotions to Heaven, seldom fail in a morning of surveying the condition of their accounts, and giving their orders to their bookkeepers and agents for the management of their respective trades; after which, being dressed in a modest garb, without any footmen or attendants, they go about their business to the Custom House, Bank, Exchange, &c., and after dinner sometimes apply themselves to business again; but the morning is much the busiest part of the day. In the evening of every other day the post comes in, when the perusing their letters may employ part of their time, as the answering them does on other days of the week; and they frequently meet at the tavern in the evening, either to transact their affairs, or to take a cheerful glass after the business of the day is over.

As to the wives and daughters of the merchants and principal tradesmen, they endeavour to imitate the Court ladies in their dress, and follow much the same diversions; and it is not uncommon to see a nobleman match with a citizen's daughter, by which she gains a title, and he discharges the incumbrances on his estate with her fortune. Merchants' sons are sometimes initiated into the same business their fathers follow; but if they find an estate gotten to their hands, many of them choose rather to become country gentlemen.

As to the lawyers or barristers, these also are frequently the younger sons of good families; and the elder brother too is sometimes entered of the Inns of Court, that he may know enough of the law to keep his estate.

A lawyer of parts and good elocution seldom fails of rising to preferment, and acquiring an estate even while he is a young man. I do not know any profession in London where a person makes his fortune so soon as in the law, if he be an eminent pleader. Several of them have of late years been advanced to the peerage; as Finch, Somers, Cowper, Harcourt, Trevor, Parker, Lechmere, King, Raymond, &c., scarce any of them much exceeding forty years of age when they arrived at that honour.

The fees are so great, and their business so engrosses every minute of their time, that it is impossible their expenses should equal their income; but it must be confessed they labour very hard, are forced to be up early and late, and to try their constitutions to the utmost (I mean those in full business) in the service of their clients. They rise in winter long before it is light, to read over their briefs; dress, and prepare themselves for the business of the day; at eight or nine they go to Westminster, where they attend and plead either in the Courts of Equity or Common Law, ordinarily till one or two, and (upon a great trial) sometimes till the evening. By that time they have got home, and dined, they have other briefs to peruse, and they are to attend the hearings, either at the Lord Chancellor's or the Rolls, till eight or nine in the evening; after which, when they return to their chambers, they are attended by their clients, and have their several cases and briefs to read over and consider that evening, or the next morning before daylight; insomuch that they have scarce time for their meals, or their natural rest, particularly at the latter end of a term. They are not always in this hurry; indeed, if they were, the best constitution must soon be worn out; nor would anyone submit to such hardships who had a subsistence, but with a prospect of acquiring a great estate suddenly; for the gold comes tumbling into the pockets of these great lawyers, which makes them refuse no cause, how intricate or doubtful soever. And this brings me to consider the high fees that are usually taken by an eminent counsel; as for a single opinion upon a case, two, three, four, and five guineas; upon a hearing, five or ten; and perhaps a great many more; and if the cause does not come on till the next day, they are all to be fee'd again, though there are not less than six or seven counsel of a side.

The next considerable profession therefore I shall mention in London is that of the physicians, who are not so numerous as the former; but those who are eminent amongst them acquire estates equal to the lawyers, though they seldom arrive at the like honours. It is a useful observation, indeed, as to English physicians, that they seldom get their bread till they have no teeth to eat it: though, when they have acquired a reputation, they are as much followed as the great lawyers; they take care, however, not to be so much fatigued. You find them at Batson's or Child's Coffee House usually in the morning, and they visit their patients in the afternoon. Those that are men of figure amongst them will not rise out of their beds or break their rest on every call. The greatest fatigue they undergo is the going up forty or fifty pair of stairs every day; for the patient is generally laid pretty near the garret, that he may not be disturbed.

These physicians are allowed to be men of skill in their profession, and well versed in other parts of learning. The great grievance here (as in the law) is that the inferior people are undone by the exorbitance of their fees; and what is still a greater hardship is, that if a physician has been employed, he must be continued, however unable the patient is to bear the expense, as no apothecary may administer anything to the sick man, if he has been prescribed to first by a physician: so that the patient is reduced to this dilemma, either to die of the disease, or starve his family, if his sickness happens to be of any duration. A physician here scorns to touch any other metal but gold, and the surgeons are still more unreasonable; and this may be one reason why the people of this city have so often recourse to quacks, for they are cheap and easily come at, and the mob are not judges of their ability; they pretend to great things; they have cured princes, and persons of the first quality, as they pretend; and it must be confessed their patients are as credulous as they can desire, taken with grand pretences, and the assurance of the impostor, and frequently like things the better that are offered them out of the common road.

I come in the next place to treat of attorneys' clerks, apprentices, inferior tradesmen, coachmen, porters, servants, and the lowest class of men in this town, which are far the most numerous: and first of the lawyers' clerks and apprentices, I find it a general complaint that they are under no manner of government; before their times are half out, they set up for gentlemen; they dress, they drink, they game, frequent the playhouses, and intrigue with the women; and it is no uncommon thing with clerks to bully their masters, and desert their service for whole days and nights whenever they see fit.

As to the ordinary tradesmen, they live by buying and selling; I cannot say they are so eminent for their probity as the merchants and tradesmen of the first rate; they seem to have a wrong bias given them in their education; many of them have no principles of honour, no other rule to go by than the fishmonger, namely, to get what they can, who consider only the weakness or ignorance of the customer, and make their demands accordingly, taking sometimes half the price they ask. And I must not forget the numbers of poor creatures who live and maintain their families by buying provisions in one part of the town, and retailing them in another, whose stock perhaps does not amount to more than forty or fifty shillings, and part of this they take up (many of them) on their clothes at a pawnbroker's on a Monday morning, which they make shift to redeem on a Saturday night, that they may appear in a proper habit at their parish-churches on a Sunday. These are the people that cry fish, fruit, herbs, roots, news, &c, about town.

As to hackney-coachmen, carmen, porters, chairmen, and watermen, though they work hard, they generally eat and drink well, and are decently clothed on holidays; for the wife, if she be industrious, either by her needle, washing, or other business proper to her sex, makes no small addition to their gains; and by their united labours they maintain their families handsomely if they have their healths.

As to the common menial servants, they have great wages, are well kept and clothed, but are, notwithstanding the plague, of almost every house in town. They form themselves into societies, or rather confederacies, contributing to the maintenance of each other when out of place; and if any of them cannot manage the family where they are entertained as they please, immediately they give notice they will be gone. There is no speaking to them; they are above correction; and if a master should attempt it, he may expect to be handsomely drubbed by the creature he feeds and harbours, or perhaps an action brought against him for it. It is become a common saying, "If my servant ben't a thief, if he be but honest, I can bear with other things;" and indeed it is very rare in London to meet with an honest servant.

When I was treating of tradesmen, I had forgot to mention those nuisances of the town, the itinerant pedlars who deal in toys and hardware, and those who pretend to sell foreign silks, linen, India handkerchiefs, and other prohibited and unaccustomed goods. These we meet at every coffee-house and corner of the streets, and they visit also every private house; the women have such a gust for everything that is foreign or prohibited, that these vermin meet with a good reception everywhere. The ladies will rather buy home manufactures of these people than of a neighbouring shopkeeper, under the pretence of buying cheaper, though they frequently buy damaged goods, and pay a great deal dearer for them than they would do in a tradesman's shop, which is a great discouragement to the fair dealer that maintains a family, and is forced to give a large credit, while these people run away with the ready money. And I am informed that some needy tradesmen employ fellows to run hawking about the streets with their goods, and sell pennyworths, in order to furnish themselves with a little money.

As to the recreations of the citizens, many of them are entertained in the same manner as the quality are, resorting to the play, park, music-meetings, &c.; and in the summer they visit Richmond, Hampstead, Epsom, and other neighbouring towns, where horse-racing, and all manner of rural sports, as well as other diversions, are followed in the summer season.

Towards autumn, when the town is thin, many of the citizens who deal in a wholesale way visit the distant parts of the kingdom to get in their debts, or procure orders for fresh parcels of goods; and much about the same time the lawyers are either employed in the several circuits, or retired to their country seats; so that the Court, the nobility and gentry, the lawyers, and many of the citizens being gone into the country, the town resumes another face. The west end of it appears perfectly deserted; in other parts their trade falls off; but still in the streets about the Royal Exchange we seldom fail to meet with crowds of people, and an air of business in the hottest season.

I have heard it affirmed, however, that many citizens live beyond their income, which puts them upon tricking and prevaricating in their dealings, and is the principal occasion of those frequent bankruptcies seen in the papers; ordinary tradesmen drink as much wine, and eat as well, as gentlemen of estates; their cloth, their lace, their linen, are as fine, and they change it as often; and they frequently imitate the quality in their expensive pleasures.

As to the diversions of the inferior tradesmen and common people on Sundays and other holidays, they frequently get out of town; the neighbouring villas are full of them, and the public-houses there usually provide a dinner in expectation of their city guests; but if they do not visit them in a morning, they seldom fail of walking out in the fields in the afternoon; every walk, every public garden and path near the town are crowded with the common people, and no place more than the park; for which reason I presume the quality are seldom seen there on a Sunday, though the meanest of them are so well dressed at these times that nobody need be ashamed of their company on that account; for you will see every apprentice, every porter, and cobbler, in as good cloth and linen as their betters; and it must be a very poor woman that has not a suit of Mantua silk, or something equal to it, to appear abroad in on holidays.

And now, if we survey these several inhabitants in one body, it will be found that there are about a million of souls in the whole town, of whom there may be 150,000 men and upwards capable of bearing arms, that is, between eighteen and sixty.

If it be demanded what proportion that part of the town properly called the City of London bears to the rest, I answer that, according to the last calculations, there are in the city 12,000 houses; in the parishes without the walls, 36,320; in the parishes of Middlesex and Surrey, which make part of the town, 46,300; and in the city and liberties of Westminster, 28,330; in which are included the precincts of the Tower, Norton Folgate, the Rolls, Whitefriars, the Inns of Court and Chancery, the King's palaces, and all other extra-parochial places.

As to the number of inhabitants in each of these four grand divisions, if we multiply the number of houses in the City of London by eight and a half, there must be 102,000 people there, according to this estimate. By the same rule, there must be 308,720 people in the seventeen parishes without the walls; 393,550 in the twenty-one out-parishes of Middlesex and Surrey; and 240,805 in the city and liberties of Westminster, all which compose the sum-total of 1,045,075 people.

Let me now proceed to inquire into the state of the several great trading companies in London. The first, in point of time, I find to be the Hamburg Company, originally styled "Merchants of the Staple" (that is, of the staple of wool), and afterwards Merchant Adventurers. They were first incorporated in the reign of King Edward I., anno 1296, and obtained leave of John, Duke of Brabant, to make Antwerp their staple or mart for the Low Countries, where the woollen manufactures then flourished more than in any country in Europe. The business of this company at first seems to be chiefly, if not altogether, the vending of English wool unwrought.

Queen Elizabeth enlarged the trade of the Company of Adventurers, and empowered them to treat with the princes and states of Germany for a place which might be the staple or mart for the woollen manufactures they exported, which was at length fixed at Hamburg, from whence they obtained the name of the Hamburg Company. They had another mart or staple also assigned them for the sale of their woollen cloths in the Low Countries, *viz.*, Dort, in Holland.

This company consists of a governor, deputy-governor, and fellowship, or court of assistants, elected annually in June, who have a power of making bye-laws for the regulation of their trade; but this trade in a manner lies open, every merchant trading thither on his own bottom, on paying an inconsiderable sum to the company; so that though the trade to Germany may be of consequence, yet the Hamburg Company, as a company, have very little advantage by their being incorporated.

The Hamburg or German Merchants export from England broad-cloth, druggets, long-ells, serges, and several sorts of stuffs, tobacco, sugar, ginger, East India goods, tin, lead, and several other commodities, the consumption of which is in Lower Germany.

England takes from them prodigious quantities of linen, linen-yarn, kid-skins, tin-plates, and a great many other commodities.

The next company established was that of the Russia Merchants, incorporated 1st and 2nd of Philip and Mary, who were empowered to trade to all lands, ports, and places in the dominions of the Emperor of Russia, and to all other lands not then discovered or frequented, lying on the north, north-east, or north-west.

The Russia Company, as a company, are not a very considerable body at present; the trade thither being carried on by private merchants, who are admitted into this trade on payment of five pounds for that privilege.

It consists of a governor, four consuls, and twenty-four assistants, annually chosen on the 1st of March.

The Russia Merchants export from England some coarse cloth, long-ells, worsted stuffs, tin, lead, tobacco, and a few other commodities.

England takes from Russia hemp, flax, linen cloth, linen yarn, Russia leather, tallow, furs, iron, potashes, &c., to an immense value.

The next company is the Eastland Company, formerly called Merchants of Elbing, a town in Polish Prussia, to the eastward of Dantzic, being the port they principally resorted to in the infancy of their trade. They were incorporated 21 Elizabeth, and empowered to trade to all countries within the Sound, Norway, Sweden, Poland, Liefland, Prussia, and Pomerania, from the river Oder eastward, *viz.*, with Riga, Revel, Konigsberg, Elbing, Dantzic, Copenhagen, Elsinore, Finland, Gothland, Eastland, and Bornholm (except Narva, which was then the only Russian port in the Baltic). And by the said patent the Eastland Company and Hamburg Company were each of them authorised to trade separately to Mecklenburg, Gothland, Silesia, Moravia, Lubeck, Wismar, Restock, and the whole river Oder.

This company consists of a governor, deputy-governor, and twenty-four assistants, elected annually in October; but either they have no power to exclude others from trading within their limits, or the fine for permission is so inconsiderable, that it can never hinder any merchants trading thither who is inclined to it; and, in fact, this trade, like the former, is carried on by private merchants, and the trade to Norway and Sweden is laid open by Act of Parliament.

To Norway and Denmark merchants send guineas, crown-pieces, bullion, a little tobacco, and a few coarse woollens.

They import from Norway, &c., vast quantities of deal boards, timber, spars, and iron.

Sweden takes from England gold and silver, and but a small quantity of the manufactures and production of England.

England imports from Sweden near two-thirds of the iron wrought up or consumed in the kingdom, copper, boards, plank, &c.

The Turkey or Levant Company was first incorporated in the reign of Queen Elizabeth, and their privileges were confirmed and enlarged in the reign of King James I., being empowered to trade to the Levant, or eastern part of the Mediterranean, particularly to Smyrna, Aleppo, Constantinople, Cyprus, Grand Cairo, Alexandria, &c. It consists of a governor, deputy-governor, and eighteen assistants or directors, chosen annually, &c. This trade is open also to every merchant paying a small consideration, and carried on accordingly by private men.

These merchants export to Turkey chiefly broadcloth, long-ells, tins, lead, and some iron; and the English merchants frequently buy up French and Lisbon sugars and transport thither, as well as bullion from Cadiz.

The commodities received from thence are chiefly raw silk, grogram yarn, dyeing stuffs of sundry kinds, drugs, soap; leather, cotton, and some fruit, oil, &c.

The East India Company were incorporated about the 42nd of Elizabeth, anno 1600, and empowered to trade to all countries to the eastward of the Cape of Good Hope, exclusive of all others.

About the middle of King William's reign it was generally said their patent was illegal, and that the Crown could not restrain the English merchants from trading to any country they were disposed to deal with; and application being made to Parliament for leave to lay the trade open, the ministry took the hint, and procured an Act of Parliament (9 and 10 William III., cap. 44) empowering every subject of England to trade to India who should raise a sum of money for the supply of the Government in proportion to the sum he should advance, and each subscriber was to have an annuity after the rate of 8 per cent. per annum, to commence from Michaelmas, 1698. And his Majesty was empowered to incorporate the subscribers, as he afterwards did, and they were usually called the New East India Company, the old company being allowed a certain time to withdraw their effects. But the old company being masters of all the towns and forts belonging to the English on the coast of India, and their members having subscribed such considerable sums towards the two millions intended to be raised, that they could not be excluded from the trade, the new company found it necessary to unite with the old company, and to trade with one joint stock, and have ever since been styled "The United Company of Merchants trading to the East Indies."

The company have a governor, deputy-governor, and twenty-four assistants or directors, elected annually in April.

The East India Company export great quantities of bullion, lead, English cloth, and some other goods, the product or manufacture of that kingdom, and import from China and India tea, china ware, cabinets, raw and wrought silks, coffee, muslins, calicoes, and other goods.

Bengal raw silk is bought at very low prices there, and is very useful in carrying on the manufactures of this kingdom.

China silk is of excellent staple, and comes at little above one-third of the price of Italian Piedmont silk.

The China silk is purchased at Canton, but their fine silk is made in the provinces of Nankin and Chekiam, where their fine manufactures are carried on, and where prodigious quantities of raw silk are made, and the best in all China.

The Royal African Company was incorporated 14 Charles II., and empowered to trade from Sallee, in South Barbary, to the Cape of Good Hope, being all the western coast of Africa. It carries no money out, and not only supplies the English plantations with servants, but brings in a great deal of bullion for those that are sold to the Spanish West Indies, besides gold dust and other commodities, as red wood, elephants' teeth, Guinea grain, &c., some of which are re-exported. The supplying the plantations with negroes is of that extraordinary advantage, that the planting sugar and tobacco and carrying on trade there could not be supported without them; which plantations are the great causes of the increase of the riches of the kingdom.

The Canary Company was incorporated in the reign of King Charles II., anno 1664, being empowered to trade to the Seven Islands, anciently called the Fortunate, and now the Canary Islands.

They have a governor, deputy-governor, and thirteen assistants or directors, chosen annually in March. This company exports baize, kerseys, serges, Norwich stuffs, and other woollen manufactures; stockings, hats, fustians, haberdashery wares, tin, and hardware; as also herrings, pilchards, salted flesh, and grain; linens, pipe-staves, hoops, &c. Importing in return Canary wines, logwood, hides, indigo, cochineal, and other commodities, the produce of America and the West Indies.

There is another company I had almost overlooked, called the Hudson's Bay Company; and though these merchants make but little noise, I find it is a very advantageous trade. They by charter trade, exclusively of all other his Britannic Majesty's subjects, to the north-west; which was granted, as I have been told, on account that they should attempt a passage by those seas to China, &c., though nothing appears now to be less their regard; nay; if all be true, they are the very people that discourage and impede all attempts made by others for the opening that passage to the South Seas. They export some woollen goods and haberdashery wares, knives, hatchets, arms, and other hardware; and in return bring back chiefly beaver-skins, and other skins and furs.

The last, and once the most considerable of all the trading companies, is that of the South Sea, established by Act of Parliament in the ninth year of the late Queen Anne; but, what by reason of the mismanagement of its directors in 1720, the miscarriage of their whale-fishery, and the intrigues of the Spaniards, their credit is sunk, and their trade has much decreased.

I proceed, in the next place, to inquire what countries the merchants of London trade to separately, not being incorporated or subject to the control of any company.

Among which is the trade to Italy, whither are exported broad-cloth, long-ells, baize, druggets, callimancoes, camlets, and divers other stuffs; leather, tin, lead, great quantities of fish, as pilchards, herrings, salmon, Newfoundland cod, &c., pepper, and other East India goods.

The commodities England takes from them are raw, thrown, and wrought silk, wine, oil, soap, olives, some dyer's wares, anchovies, &c.

To Spain the merchants export broad-cloth, druggets, callimancoes, baize, stuff of divers kinds, leather, fish, tin, lead, corn, &c.

The commodities England takes from them are wine, oil, fruit of divers kinds, wool, indigo, cochineal, and dyeing stuffs.

To Portugal also are exported broad-cloth, druggets, baize, long-ells, callimancoes, and all other sorts of stuffs; as well as tin, lead, leather, fish, corn, and other English commodities.

England takes from them great quantities of wine, oil, salt, and fruit, and gold, both in bullion and specie; though it is forfeited, if seized in the ports of Portugal.

The French take very little from England in a fair way, dealing chiefly with owlers, or those that clandestinely export wool and fuller's-earth, &c. They indeed buy some of our tobacco, sugar, tin, lead, coals, a few stuffs, serges, flannels, and a small matter of broad-cloth.

England takes from France wine, brandy, linen, lace, fine cambrics, and cambric lawns, to a prodigious value; brocades, velvets, and many other rich silk manufactures, which are either run, or come by way of Holland; the humour of some of the nobility and gentry being such, that although they have those manufactures made as good at home, if not better than abroad, yet they are forced to be called by the name of French to make them sell. Their linens are run in very great quantities, as are their wine and brandy, from the Land's End even to the Downs.

To Flanders are exported serges, a few flannels, a very few stuffs, sugar, tobacco, tin, and lead.

England takes from them fine lace, fine cambrics, and cambric-lawns, Flanders whited linens, threads, tapes, incles, and divers other commodities, to a very great value.

To Holland the merchants export broad-cloth, druggets, long-ells, stuffs of a great many sorts, leather, corn, coals, and something of almost every kind that this kingdom produces; besides all sorts of India and Turkey re-exported goods, sugars, tobacco, rice, ginger, pitch and tar, and sundry other commodities of the produce of our American plantations.

England takes from Holland great quantities of fine Holland linen, threads, tapes, and incles; whale fins, brass battery, madder, argol, with a large number of other commodities and toys; clapboard, wainscot, &c.

To Ireland are exported fine broad-cloth, rich silks, ribbons, gold and silver lace, manufactured iron and cutlery wares, pewter, great quantities of hops, coals, dyeing wares, tobacco, sugar, East India goods, raw silk, hollands, and almost everything they use, but linens, coarse woollens, and eatables.

England takes from Ireland woollen yarn, linen yarn, great quantities of wool in the fleece, and some tallow.

They have an extraordinary trade for their hides, tallow; beef, butter, &c., to Holland, Flanders, France, Portugal, and Spain, which enables them to make large remittances.

To the sugar plantations are exported all sorts of clothing, both linen, silks, and woollen; wrought iron, brass, copper, all sorts of household furniture, and a great part of their food.

They return sugar, ginger, and several commodities, and all the bullion and gold they can meet with, but rarely carry out any.

To the tobacco plantations are exported clothing, household goods, iron manufactures of all sorts, saddles, bridles, brass and copper wares; and notwithstanding they dwell among the woods, they take their very turnery wares, and almost everything else that may be called the manufacture of England.

England takes from them not only what tobacco is consumed at home, but very great quantities for re-exportation.

To Carolina are exported the same commodities as to the tobacco plantations. This country lying between the 32nd and 36th degrees of northern latitude, the soil is generally fertile. The rice it produces is said to be the best in the world; and no country affords better silk than has been brought from thence, though for want of sufficient encouragement the quantity imported is very small. It is said both bohea and green tea have been raised there, extraordinary good of the kind. The olive-tree grows wild, and thrives very well, and might soon be improved so far as to supply us with large quantities of oil. It is said the fly from whence the cochineal is made is found very common, and if care was taken very great quantities might be made. The indigo plant grows exceedingly well. The country has plenty of iron mines in it, and would produce excellent hemp and flax, if encouragement was given for raising it.

To Pennsylvania are exported broad-cloth, kerseys, druggets, serges, and manufactures of all kinds.

To New England are exported all sorts of woollen manufactures, linen, sail-cloth and cordage for rigging their ships, haberdashery, &c. They carry lumber and provisions to the sugar plantations; and exchange provisions for logwood with the logwood-cutters at Campeachy. They send pipe and barrel-staves and fish to Spain, Portugal, and the Straits. They send pitch, tar, and turpentine to England, with some skins.

Having considered the trading companies, and other branches of foreign trade, I shall now inquire into the establishment of the Bank of England.

The governor and company of the Bank of England, &c., are enjoined not to trade, or suffer any person in trust for them to trade, with any of the stock, moneys or effects, in the buying or selling of any merchandise or goods whatsoever, on pain of forfeiting the treble value. Yet they may deal in bills of exchange, and in buying and selling of bullion, gold or silver, or in selling goods mortgaged to them, and not redeemed at the time agreed on, or within three months after, or such goods as should be the produce of lands purchased by the corporation. All bills obligatory and of credit under the seal of the corporation made to any person, may by endorsement be assigned, and such assignment shall transfer the property to the moneys due upon the same, and the assignee may sue in his own name.

There is at present due to this Bank
from the Government on the original
fund at 6 pounds per cent. 1,600,000 (pounds)
For cancelling of Exchequer bills,
3 George I 1,500,000
Purchased of the South Sea Company 4,000,000

Annuities at 4 pounds per cent. charged
on the duty on coals since
Lady Day, 1719. 1,750,000
Ditto, charged on the surplus of
the funds for the lottery of 1714 1,250,000
Total due to the Bank of England 10,100,000 (pounds)

Give me leave to observe here, that most of the foreign trade of this town is transacted by brokers, of which there are three sorts, *viz.*, 1st, Exchange-brokers, 2ndly, brokers for goods and merchandise, and 3rdly, ship-brokers.

The exchange-brokers, who are versed in the course of exchange, furnish the merchant with money or bills, as he has occasion for either.

The broker of goods lets the merchant know where he may furnish himself with them, and the settled price; or if he wants to sell, where he may meet with a chapman for his effects.

The ship-broker finds ships for the merchant, when he wants to send his goods abroad; or goods for captains and masters of vessels to freight their ships with.

If it be demanded what share of foreign trade London hath with respect to the rest of the kingdom; it seems to have a fourth part of the whole, at least if we may judge by the produce of the customs, which are as three to twelve, or thereabouts.

As to the manufactures carried on in the City of London; here mechanics have acquired a great deal of reputation in the world, and in many things not without reason; for they excel in clock and cabinet-work, in making saddles, and all sorts of tools, and other things. The door and gun locks, and fire-arms, are nowhere to be paralleled; the silk manufacture is equal to that of France, or any other country, and is prodigiously enlarged of late years. Dyers also are very numerous in and about London, and are not exceeded by any foreigners in the beauty or durableness of their colours: and those that print and stain cottons and linens have brought that art to great perfection. Printers of books, also, may equal those abroad; but the best paper is imported from other countries.

The manufacture of glass here is equal to that of Venice, or any other country in Europe, whether we regard the coach or looking-glasses, perspective, drinking-glasses, or any other kind of glass, whatever. The making of pins and needles is another great manufacture in this town, as is that of wire-drawings of silver, gold, and other metals. The goldsmiths and silversmiths excel in their way. The pewterers and brasiers furnish all manner of vessels and implements for the kitchen, which are as neatly and substantially made and furnished here as in any country in Europe. The trades of hat-making and shoe-making employ multitudes of mechanics; and the tailors are equally numerous. The cabinet, screen, and chair-makers contribute also considerably to the adorning and furnishing the dwelling-house. The common smiths, bricklayers, and carpenters are no inconsiderable branch of mechanics; as may well be imagined in a town of this magnitude, where so many churches, palaces, and private buildings are continually repairing, and so many more daily erecting upon new foundations. And this brings me to mention the shipwrights, who are employed in the east part of the town, on both sides the river Thames, in building ships, lighters, boats, and other vessels; and the coopers, who make all the casks for domestic and foreign service. The anchorsmiths, ropemakers, and others employed in the rigging and fitting out ships, are very numerous; and brewing and distilling may be introduced among the manufactures of this town, where so many thousand quarters of malt are annually converted into beer and spirits: and as the various kinds of beer brewed here are not to be paralleled in the world, either for quantity or quality, so the distilling of spirits is brought to such perfection that the best of them are not easily to be distinguished from French brandy.

Having already mentioned ship-building among the mechanic trades, give me leave to observe farther, that in this England excels all other nations; the men-of-war are the most beautiful as well as formidable machines that ever floated on the ocean.

As to the number of foreigners in and about this great city, there cannot be given any certain account, only this you may depend upon, that there are more of the French nation than of any other: such numbers of them coming over about the time of the Revolution and since to avoid the persecution of Louis XIV., and so many more to get their bread, either in the way of trade, or in the service of persons of quality; and I find they have upwards of twenty churches in this town, to each of which, if we allow 1,000 souls, then their number must be at least 20,000. Next to the French nation I account most of the Dutch and Germans; for there are but few Spaniards or Portuguese, and the latter are generally Jews; and except the raree-show men, we see scarce any of the natives of Italy here; though the Venetian and some other Italian princes have their public chapels here for the exercise of the Romish religion.

Printed in Great Britain
by Amazon

61257977R00050